Rail Blue

Paul Shannon

Ian Allan
PUBLISHING

Dedication
To my mother

First published 2010

ISBN 978 0 7110 3425 9

© Ian Allan Publishing Ltd 2010

Published by Ian Allan Publishing

an imprint of Ian Allan Publishing Ltd, Hersham, Surrey KT12 4RG.
Printed in England by Ian Allan Printing Ltd, Hersham, Surrey KT12 4RG.

Distributed in the United States of America and Canada by BookMasters Distribution Services.

Visit the Ian Allan Publishing website at www.ianallanpublishing.com

Mixed Sources
Product group from well-managed forests and other controlled sources
www.fsc.org Cert no. SGS-COC-005526
© 1996 Forest Stewardship Council
FSC

Front cover: Rated 'Class 1' but scarcely meriting Inter-City status, train 1G29, the 12.41 football supporters' special from Sunderland to Middlesbrough, passes Seaham on 14 November 1981 behind No 37 109. This was the second of three Sunderland–Middlesbrough specials on that date, all locomotive-hauled. No 37 109 was to survive in EWS ownership until 2007, when it was purchased by the East Lancashire Railway. *Paul Shannon*

Previous page: A small pool of Class 50s remained on the London Midland Region for a time after the 'Electric Scots' scheme was completed in 1974. No 50 040 stands at Wigan Wallgate station with a diverted Glasgow–Manchester express in September 1975. This train was running via Wigan, entailing reversals at Lostock Junction and Wallgate, because of engineering work on its booked route via Bolton. *David Cross*

Above: Taking a rest from their weekday freight operations at Edge Hill stabling point on Sunday 11 November 1973 are Class 40 locomotives Nos 321, 40 175 and 310, together with Class 47 No 1521. The three Class 40s were allocated to Longsight, but the Class 47 was a Gateshead machine, having possibly reached Liverpool on a trans-Pennine express. *Brian Roberts*

Contents

Above: For many years the Class 46 'Peaks' were shared between Western and Eastern Region depots, but by late 1981 all surviving members of the class were allocated to Gateshead. No 46 023 heads south at Plawsworth on 29 October 1981 with train 6O34, the 12.45 Tyne Yard–Ridham Dock merry-go-round working, conveying coal for the Bowaters paper mill at Sittingbourne. *Paul Shannon*

Acknowledgements

I am grateful to those photographers who loaned historic material for inclusion in this book and to David Rapson for advice on the manuscript.

Bibliography

Geoffrey Freeman Allen: *British Railfreight Today and Tomorrow* (Jane's, 1984)

S. K. Baker: *Rail Atlas of Great Britain and Ireland*, various editions (Oxford Publishing Co)

Geoffrey Body: *Britain's Rail Routes Past and Present: The East Coast Main Line* (Silver Link Publishing, 1995)

David N. Clough and D. I. Rapson: *Locomotive Recognition: Class 37s* (Ian Allan Publishing, 1991)

Michael J. Collins: *Life and Times: Freightliner* (Oxford Publishing Co, 1991)

Brian Reed: *Diesel-hydraulic Locomotives of the Western Region* (David & Charles, 1974)

Michael Rhodes: *British Marshalling Yards* (Oxford Publishing Co, 1988)

Michael Rhodes and Paul Shannon: *Freight Only* volumes 1, 2 and 3 (Silver Link Publishing, 1987/8)

Paul Shannon: *Rail Freight Since 1968: Wagonload, Coal, Bulk Freight* (Silver Link Publishing, 2006/8)

David St John Thomas and Patrick Whitehouse: *BR in the Eighties* (David & Charles, 1990)

M. Vincent and C. Green: *The InterCity Story* (Oxford Publishing Co, 1994)

abc British Railways Locomotives and Other Motive Power, various editions (Ian Allan Publishing)

British Railways Pre-Grouping Atlas and Gazetteer (Ian Allan Publishing)

Locoshed Book, various editions (Ian Allan Publishing)

Various issues of *Modern Railways, Rail Enthusiast, The Railway Magazine, Railway Observer* and *Railway World*

Introduction

This book looks back at a period of railway history that many people considered mind-numbingly drab. From the mid-1960s until the early 1980s uniformity was almost an obsession on a railway system that was trying hard to create a new, forward-looking image and forget the past. Out went the green and maroon liveries that had adorned most of Britain's locomotives and coaching stock since the 1950s; the new corporate colour was blue.

The basis of the new livery was the model rake of 'XP64' stock hauled by a Brush Type 4 locomotive that had been outshopped from Derby in 1964. The locomotive wore all-over turquoise blue with red panels on the cab sides, while the carriages were finished in a combination of turquoise blue and pale grey. After much deliberation, during which a slightly darker shade of blue was chosen and the red panels were abandoned, BR decreed in June 1966 that all new locomotives and stock would carry the new livery, and that existing vehicles would be repainted as soon as practicable. The transition period was lengthy — a few main-line locomotives still wore green in the late 1970s — but eventually the transformation was complete, even including the three narrow-gauge steam locomotives operating the BR-owned Vale of Rheidol Railway.

Strictly speaking, there were two versions of corporate blue livery. All-over plain blue was applied to all locomotives, to all parcels and newspaper stock, to the small fleet of suburban locomotive-hauled coaches, and to most types of diesel and electric multiple-unit. Blue and grey was used for most passenger-carrying hauled stock, for mail vans and for a few classes of multiple-unit designed for long-distance journeys. In the 1980s the use of blue and grey on multiple-units became more widespread, plain blue being retained only on certain types with a limited life expectancy, such as the Cravens Class 105 and the Birmingham Class 104.

The very first blue-liveried locomotives had small yellow warning panels on their cabs, but by the early 1970s BR had opted for cleaner-looking — and safer — full yellow ends. Those locomotives still in green were also given full yellow ends as an interim measure. Any extra embellishments that staff were tempted to apply, such as red buffer beams, were frowned upon. Even the time-honoured practice of naming locomotives was outlawed — though this policy was later relaxed following the naming of No 87 001 as *Stephenson* in 1976.

The corporate identity wasn't just about the blue (and blue-and-grey) livery. It featured BR's double-arrow symbol – surely one of the most striking and successful logos of all time, and still in use today on our fragmented railway system as an unmistakable label for a railway station. It also introduced a custom-designed alphabet by Jock Kinneir, closely based on the Helvetica typeface but with an evening up of the difference between 'thick' and 'thin' strokes. The double-arrow symbol and BR typeface soon adorned not only station platforms and buildings but also posters, notices, timetables and other printed matter.

While the corporate identity was establishing itself other changes manifested themselves across the railway system. The practice of displaying train headcodes was abolished in January 1976 because the widespread use of visual displays in power signalboxes made them unnecessary. As locomotives passed through depots for minor examinations their headcodes were set permanently at '0O00', and the headcode selector and operating handles were removed. In due course many locomotives had their headcode panels plated over. New locomotive builds such as Classes 56 and 87 had no headcode panels.

The Rail-blue period saw major changes to railway infrastructure. The decline of wagonload freight with its requirement for shunting and trip working meant that many yards, sidings and loops could be closed. On both passenger and freight routes dozens of signalboxes were closed and their semaphore signals removed, either as a result of multiple-aspect resignalling schemes or because of declining traffic levels. Some sections of railway were reduced to single track as an economy measure, a policy which would sometimes cause operational headaches when traffic levels later recovered. And many stations had their dilapidated Victorian architecture replaced by utilitarian structures of varying quality, including the minimalist 'bus shelters' provided at unstaffed halts.

From a 21st-century perspective the Rail-blue period was short. The first major challenge to uniformity came in 1977, when Stratford depot outshopped two Class 47 locomotives with silver roofs, red buffer-beams and bodyside Union flags for the Queen's Silver Jubilee. Silver roofs became a feature of Stratford locomotives. Before long, locomotives of various classes sported large logos and large bodyside numbers. And then in the early 1980s the formation of BR's business sectors brought the beginning of the end of the corporate image. However, unadorned Rail blue took a long time to disappear: the majority of the Class 08 shunter fleet, and a good number of Class 20, 31 and 33 locomotives retained blue livery into the 1990s. Today, the once reviled corporate livery evokes its own nostalgia, as demonstrated by the painting of some preserved diesels in blue.

Class 55 'Deltics' worked the East Coast leg of cross-country services in addition to their main Inter-City duties to and from King's Cross. No 55 017 *The Durham Light Infantry* approaches Newcastle station on 13 September 1980 with the 09.50 Edinburgh–Plymouth, which it would haul as far as York. Heading north on the adjacent track is 'Peak' No 46 014 with empty Mk 1 coaching stock. *Paul Shannon*

Inter-City

Although back in 1950 British Railways gave the name 'Inter-City' to one of its express services between London Paddington and Wolverhampton, it was not until the mid-1960s that the term entered general use to describe the network of fast passenger services linking major towns and cities. A decisive moment was the launch in April 1966 of electric services on the West Coast main line from Euston to Manchester and Liverpool, which were branded 'Inter-City' to market their speeds of up to 100mph and their regular-interval timetable. Gradually the title became an instantly recognisable label for a particular type of rail service, not just in the UK but also in mainland Europe and many other parts of the world.

The Beeching report of 1963 had identified inter-city (without capital letters) traffic as a growth area, in contrast to the gloomy prognosis for many rural services. The modernisation of the West Coast main line had started well before Beeching, but its completion proved the report to be right — passenger traffic rose by some 66% thanks to the new service. The Inter-City product was supported by new rolling stock, air-conditioned Mk 2d/e/f vehicles entering service from 1969 on the West Coast main line and other principal routes. Previously air-conditioning had been reserved for the prestigious 'Blue Pullman' units introduced in 1960.

Inter-City trains from Euston to London, Manchester and Liverpool used a heterogeneous fleet of electric locomotives, belonging to Classes 81-86. Some of the classes were more successful than others: Classes 83 and 84 were unreliable, spent long periods out of use and faced early withdrawal, whereas the Class 86s were the most favoured type, many examples continuing in use into the 21st century.

For the non-electrified stretch between Weaver Junction and Glasgow BR introduced its last fleet of purpose-built express passenger diesel locomotives, the Class 50s. As things turned out, the 50 Class 50s spent only a few years on the West Coast main line, as the 'Electric Scots' extension was authorised in 1970 and full electric working to Glasgow was inaugurated in 1974. For this service BR introduced 36 Class 87 electric locomotives, similar in many ways to the Class 86s but with a modest increase in maximum speed, to 110mph. As for coaching stock, the first Mk 3 vehicles entered service in 1975, giving increased levels of passenger comfort.

In the longer term the West Coast main line was set to be transformed by BR's flagship traction project, the Advanced Passenger Train. Unfortunately that particular transformation never took place. Using experience from the gas-turbine APT-E in the early 1970s, BR introduced three pre-production electric APT-P sets in 1979. However, technical problems with this revolutionary tilting train soon emerged, and funding to take the project forward was denied. Nevertheless, to say that APT-P was a complete failure would be unfair, and it would be another 20 years before Virgin's 'Pendolino' matched the Euston– Glasgow timing of 3 hours 52 minutes that was achieved by APT-P in 1984.

For Inter-City services from Euston to non-electrified destinations such as Shrewsbury, Holyhead, Blackpool and Inverness, BR standardised on Class 47/4 traction wherever possible. The '47/4s' also powered an increasing share of cross-country Inter-City trains via Birmingham — that highly diverse group of services gathered in Table 51 in the BR timetable that stretched from Aberdeen, Bradford and Liverpool to Swansea, Penzance and Poole. Not until the 1980s did Inter-City 125 units take over a share of cross-country duties.

The Midland main line out of St Pancras led a fairly quiet existence in the BR-blue period. On the core route to Nottingham, Derby and Sheffield the Class 45 'Peaks' that had replaced steam remained in charge until the arrival of IC125 units in the 1980s. However, away from the core route there were some changes. Through trains between St Pancras and Manchester were diverted via Chesterfield after the closure of the Matlock–Peak Forest route in 1968 and were withdrawn altogether in the 1970s. The much-publicised run-down of the Settle to Carlisle line began with the withdrawal of through trains from St Pancras to Scotland in 1976, followed by the loss of remaining Inter-City services in 1982.

On the East Coast main line the iconic 'Deltics' held sway on top-link services until the late 1970s. As on the West Coast route, passengers benefited from the introduction of air-conditioned Mk 2d stock. Line-speed improvements brought useful reductions in journey times: by 1967 some 77 miles of track was cleared for 100mph running, and by 1976 major infrastructure work had brought 89% of the route between King's Cross and Newcastle up to the 100mph standard. The work included straightening out curves at Offord and Newton Hall (Durham) and the remodelling of Peterborough station.

From being the poor relation of the West Coast route in the 1960s, the East Coast main line jumped higher up the investment agenda in the 1970s and benefited from IC125 operation from 1978. The relatively flat, straight permanent way between King's Cross and Newcastle lent itself to the IC125 — or High Speed Train, as it was called in its early days. Indeed, it was on the straight between York and Darlington that the prototype High Speed Train had reached an impressive top speed of 143.2mph. Once the production sets entered service Edinburgh came within five hours of London, and other journey times were correspondingly slashed. The 'Deltics' finished their career on what were misleadingly termed 'semi-fast' services between King's Cross and York (which in reality involved a succession of fast sprints) as well as on humbler duties such as Newcastle–Edinburgh locals.

On the Western Region the most striking change from the late 1960s onwards was BR's decision to abandon diesel-hydraulic traction. Although the hydraulics performed well, they were non-standard because all other regions had opted for diesel-electrics. The hydraulics represented only about 11% of the total BR main-line diesel fleet. Faced with a motive-power surplus, BR sensibly chose to eliminate whatever was non-standard. The Class 42 and 43 'Warships' were the first major hydraulic type to go, the whole fleet being withdrawn by the end of 1972. Most of the Class 35 'Hymeks' had been retired by the end of 1973, just a few soldiering on until 1975. The Class 52 'Westerns' survived rather longer; indeed, the class was fitted with train air-brake equipment, and withdrawals did not begin until 1973, the last examples bowing out in 1977.

To replace the diesel-hydraulics BR drafted in diesel-electric locomotives from other regions, including the Class 50s, which used their 100mph capability to good effect on Inter-City duties out of London Paddington. However, the diesel-electric locomotives proved to be only a stopgap. The Western Region Inter-City network was the first to benefit from BR's investment in the IC125, the first 16 trainsets entering service in October 1976 and heralding a new era of train travel.

By 1977 almost all Inter-City services on the London–Bristol and London–South Wales routes were in the hands of IC125 units, with journey times of as little as 70 minutes from Paddington to Bristol Parkway — an average speed of 96mph — and 86 minutes from Paddington to Newport. Soon further IC125s were on order for West of England services. Here too there would be reductions in journey times, even though opportunities for high-speed running in the West Country were limited. Just as big a factor as line speed was the high power-to-weight ratio of the IC125s, enabling them to accelerate fast and tackle gradients more easily than many locomotive-hauled trains. Testimony to their undoubted success is the fact that, at the time of writing, many sets are still in use with First Great Western, more than 30 years after their introduction.

The Southern Region provided fewer opportunities for true Inter-City services than did BR's other regions. Judging from the network map accompanying the BR timetable, almost all routes from London to the coast ranked as Inter-City, along with the coastal route between Portsmouth and Brighton. In reality the electric multiple-units that plied these routes offered a service that could not really be compared with the speed and comfort of IC125 units or the hauled stock on the West and East Coast main lines. Nevertheless, some trains on the Southern Region were confidently marketed as Inter-City. The commissioning of third-rail electrification to Bournemouth in 1967 heralded an Inter-City service that stretched beyond the electrified network as far as Weymouth, thanks to the introduction of '4-TC' units that could be powered by '4-REP' electric units to Bournemouth and by diesel locomotives for the rest of the journey. On the Brighton line the elderly 'Brighton Belle' Pullman units provided a premium service until their withdrawal in 1972. In a later era the intensive service between Victoria and Gatwick Airport gained Inter-City status, using cascaded air-conditioned rolling stock and Class 73 locomotives.

In East Anglia the Inter-City network included the EMU-operated service to Walton and Clacton and locomotive-hauled trains on the King's Lynn and Norwich lines, together with a sparse boat-train service to Harwich. Classes 37 and 47 were the preferred traction for the locomotive-hauled trains until the commissioning of electrification, which reached Ipswich in 1985, Norwich in 1987 and King's Lynn in 1991. The use of locomotives to Norwich was to continue after electrification, with Class 86s redeployed from the West Coast main line.

In the North of England the Trans-Pennine line via Diggle had a long-standing Inter-City association thanks to the Swindon DMU sets — later Class 124 — which were introduced on the route in 1960 with the designation 'Inter-City'. By the early 1980s, however, the Class 124s — and their Class 123 cousins, which had moved north in 1977 — were no longer meriting the Inter-City label. Under BR's sector-based reorganisation the Trans-Pennine routes would pass to Provincial.

The main Inter-City routes in Scotland included not only the Anglo-Scottish main lines but also a number of internal routes: Glasgow–Edinburgh, Glasgow/ Edinburgh–Inverness/Aberdeen and Inverness–Aberdeen. On the Glasgow– Edinburgh route Swindon 'Inter-City' DMUs gave way in May 1971 to innovative push-pull trains, using dedicated six-coach rakes of Mk 2 stock fitted with multi-core jumper cables and air pipes which enabled Class 27 locomotives coupled at each end to work in multiple. These trains were replaced in 1980 by rakes of Mk 3 stock with a Class 47/7 locomotive at one end and a driving trailer at the other. Elsewhere, the Inverness–Aberdeen service retained its Inter-City DMUs until the 1980s, whereas the longer-distance routes from the Central Belt to Inverness and Aberdeen were locomotive-operated throughout the BR-blue period.

Above: Paving the way for one of the most successful trains ever to run on Britain's railways, the prototype High Speed Train, led by power car No 41001, passes Essendine on the East Coast main line on 31 July 1973. *Geoff Plumb collection*

Below: The futuristic gas-turbine Advanced Passenger Train, APT-E, stands at the end of the Old Dalby test track at Melton Junction on 19 April 1975. Soon the train would make history by reaching a record speed of 152mph between Swindon and Reading. In June 1976 its four-year testing programme ended, and the train was then presented to the National Railway Museum at York. *Geoff Plumb collection*

Above: Entering Plymouth station on a sunny April morning in 1969 are Class 42 'Warships' Nos 866 *Zebra* and 831 *Monarch* with the 10.15 Penzance–Paddington express. By this time the first 'Warship' withdrawals had already taken effect; the entire class would be eradicated by the end of 1972. *Bernard Mills*

Below: The 08.30 from Paddington to Penzance was regularly double-headed by a 'Warship'/'Western' combination as a means of getting an extra locomotive into Cornwall. Nos 823 *Hermes* and 1011 *Western Thunderer* enter Cornwall at Saltash with this train on 2 October 1969. *Bernard Mills*

Above: Class 42 'Warship' No D841 *Roebuck* takes the Frome avoiding line at Clink Road Junction with the 07.27 from Ealing Broadway to Penzance on 12 July 1969. *Hugh Ballantyne*

Below: One of the graceful bridges across the 60ft-deep Sonning Cutting between Reading and Maidenhead sets the scene for No D1071 *Western Renown* as it heads towards the capital with a West of England express in June 1974. *I. J. Hodson*

Left: Class 52 No D1023 *Western Fusilier* awaits departure from Paddington with train 1C61, the 20.15 to Swansea, on 25 October 1973. By this time nine 'Westerns' had been withdrawn, but No D1023 was to remain in service until February 1977, after which it passed into preservation. At the time of writing it is based at the National Railway Museum, York. *David Rapson*

Below left: Although the last Class 35 'Hymeks' would not be withdrawn until 1975, on 22 September 1973 BR ran a 'Hymek Swansong' tour, hauled by Nos 7001 and 7028. The tour ran from Paddington to Hereford via the Severn Tunnel and returned to the capital via Worcester and Oxford, being seen here at Worcester Shrub Hill station. This was one of the first diesel-hauled enthusiast specials organised by BR and gave impetus to the idea of preserving a 'Hymek' locomotive. *David Rapson*

Above right: The 'Peaks' had a long association with cross-country services to the South West, members of Classes 45 and 46 running alongside Western Region diesel-hydraulics. No 45 047 is pictured near Dawlish with the 07.40 Leeds–Penzance on 24 March 1976. *Hugh Ballantyne*

Right: One of the original batch of named Western Region Class 47s, No 1662 *Isambard Kingdom Brunel* rests between duties at Severn Tunnel Junction on 19 August 1973. A few months later it would be fitted with electric train-heating supply and renumbered 47 484, enabling it to continue its Inter-City duties. Later in its life it was one of the four Class 47s to be re-liveried in lined Brunswick green for the GWR 150th-anniversary celebrations. *David Rapson*

Below: After the electrification of the West Coast main line north of Crewe BR cascaded its Class 50 fleet to the Western Region to enable withdrawal of the 'Western' hydraulics. No 50 011 stands at its new home depot of Bristol Bath Road on 20 June 1974. This locomotive would later become the first Class 50 to be withdrawn from BR stock, in February 1987. *David Rapson*

Above: Anorak-clad trainspotters grasp the opportunity to inspect the cab of IC125 power car No W43010 during its layover time at Cardiff Central on 5 February 1977. The 'W' prefix was carried because the power cars were originally numbered as coaching stock; only later were they classified as locomotives. *Paul Shannon*

Below: IC125 units brought new standards of comfort to West Country services, even if the opportunities for high-speed running were limited. Power car No 43120 leads the 16.20 Paddington–Plymouth out of Taunton station on 7 August 1982. The fine array of lower-quadrant semaphores was nearing the end of its life, multiple-aspect signalling reaching Taunton in 1986. *Paul Shannon*

Above: Rail blue was a novelty on 1 July 1967, when this combination of BRCW Type 3 No D6511 and '4-TC' trailer units was photographed passing St Denys on a Waterloo– Bournemouth service. Just eight days later steam would finish on the Bournemouth line; trains of '4-TC' stock would then be powered by '4-REP' electric units between Waterloo and Bournemouth and by Class 33 locomotives on the non-electrified stretch between Bournemouth and Weymouth. *Derek Cross*

Below: The Class 73 electro-diesels were employed mainly on freight but also appeared on boat trains and excursions on Southern Region lines. Nos 73 135 and 73 117 shunt empty Mk 1 stock at Clapham Junction on 21 September 1981. Both locomotives were to survive into the 21st century; No 73 135 was renumbered 73 235 for Gatwick Express duties and later became a standby locomotive for South West Trains, while No 73 117 was purchased by Fragonset for potential hire to other operators. *Paul Shannon*

Above: Built in 1932, the '5-BEL' 'Brighton Belle' units were the first electric Pullman stock in the world. The trains lost their umber and cream Pullman livery in the interests of maintaining BR's corporate image but continued to provide a premium service between Waterloo and Brighton until their withdrawal in 1972. Unit No 3053 stands at Waterloo ready to form the RCTS 'Brighton Belle Commemorative' special on 8 April 1972. *Laurence Waters*

Below: Regular locomotive haulage returned to the Brighton line in 1984 when BR launched its Class 73-powered Gatwick Express service. No 73 107 passes Horley with the 15.45 Victoria–Gatwick Airport on 4 July 1985. *David Rapson*

Above: Electric-train-heat Class 45/1s appeared frequently on cross-country trains to and from the North East, in addition to their core work on the Midland main line. No 45 133 passes Stone Bridge, south of Durham, with the 16.17 Newcastle–Cardiff on 12 May 1982. In the foreground is the trackbed of the erstwhile branch to Lanchester and Consett, which once made a complex junction here with the East Coast main line and with the branch to Bishop Auckland. *Paul Shannon*

Below: Although Halifax was served mainly by DMUs on the Calder Valley line, it once enjoyed a daily locomotive-hauled service to London King's Cross, routed via Huddersfield and combined with a train from Leeds at Wakefield Westgate. No 31 409 heads east near Bradley Junction with the 08.40 departure from Halifax on 27 May 1977. With a scheduled arrival time of 13.03 at King's Cross, this was not the fastest of Inter-City services! *Brian Roberts*

Above: On Monday 31 May 1982 BR ran a number of special trains in connection with the visit of Pope John Paul II to York. Passing the stabling point at Hartlepool is No 47 220 with train 1G37, the 09.52 from Newcastle to York. Locomotive-hauled extras also ran from Saltburn and Redcar. *Paul Shannon*

Below: The IC125 units used on cross-country routes had only one First-class coach, unlike those built for services out of Paddington and King's Cross, which had two. Here a cross-country set headed by power car No 43172 passes Harrowgate, near Darlington, on a southbound service on Sunday 28 February 1982. *Paul Shannon*

Above: No 45 148 passes West Hampstead Midland with a down express comprising air-conditioned stock on 6 April 1978. This locomotive was withdrawn in 1987 and was one of several Class 45s used as dead-load vehicles by the Research Department at Mickleover before heading to MC Metals in Glasgow for scrapping. *Paul Shannon*

Below: No 45 127 approaches Wigston South Junction with the 14.05 St Pancras–Nottingham on 16 April 1983, shortly before IC125 units took over most services on the Midland main line. The semaphore signals in the Leicester area were to last several more years, Leicester power 'box not being commissioned until 1986/7. *Paul Shannon*

Above: The 'Manchester Pullman' ran from 1966 until 1985 with purpose-built coaching stock based on the Mk 2 design. It was the last Pullman service to run with dedicated stock on BR. No 86 245 speeds past Milepost 141 near Norton Bridge with the down 'Manchester Pullman' on 24 May 1977. After withdrawal of the Pullman service the coaches found further employment on charters, and at the time of writing 10 examples remain in use with West Coast Railways. *Hugh Ballantyne*

Below: Suitably adorned with white wheel rims and silver buffers, No 47 449 arrives at Stafford with the Royal Train carrying the Duke of Edinburgh on 22 June 1981. The first, fourth and fifth carriages belong to the small fleet of royal vehicles converted from BR Mk 3 stock in 1977, while the second and third carriages were built in the 1950s. *Hugh Ballantyne*

Above: Already nearly 20 years old, No 86 208 *City of Chester* calls at Stoke-on-Trent with the 11.53 Manchester Piccadilly–Euston on 22 April 1985. The locomotive would remain in front-line service on the West Coast main line until the mid-1990s, later serving for a time with Rail Express Systems before withdrawal in 2000. *Paul Shannon*

Below: BR continued to run InterCity trains to and from Blackpool until 1992. No 85 018 heads north near Leighton Buzzard with the 15.05 Euston–Blackpool North on 15 July 1989. The train comprises an interesting mixture of InterCity-liveried Mk 1, blue-and-grey early Mk 2 and InterCity-liveried Mk 3 stock. *Paul Shannon*

Left: The signal gantry at Burnden Junction provides a striking backdrop for freshly repainted Class 47/4 No 47 432 as it approaches Bolton with the 16.40 from Nottingham to Barrow-in-Furness on 6 June 1983. At that time the Windsor Link between Salford and Deansgate was not yet open, so trains such as this had to follow a circuitous route across Manchester via Ashburys, Philips Park and Miles Platting. *Paul Shannon*

Below left: Its headcode panel set to 'four zeros', No 47 554 approaches Horton-in-Ribblesdale with an up express on 10 August 1977 while No 25 319 waits on the down line with an engineers' train. At this time the Settle–Carlisle line had a weekday passenger service of just three trains each way; the smaller stations such as Horton were served only by seasonal 'Dalesrail' excursion trains. *Paul Shannon*

Above right: The fifty Class 50s were built to replace steam on the northern section of the West Coast main line and operated in pairs on the heaviest trains. Nos D438 and D429 depart Carlisle with a Glasgow–Euston express on 15 May 1970. Both locomotives would end their working lives on the Western Region; No D438 was later scrapped, while No D429 became one of the 18 Class 50s that survive in preservation. *Derek Cross*

Right: Class 40 No D205 passes Crawick Viaduct, near Sanquhar, with the 15.33 Blackpool–Paisley on 11 August 1973. This locomotive was later renumbered 40 005 but would face withdrawal as early as 1976. *Derek Cross*

Above: Two batches of Class 40s were allocated to Haymarket depot from new, but No 40 184 was originally based on the London Midland Region and not transferred north of the border until 1974. It is pictured arriving at Dundee with the 23.15 King's Cross–Aberdeen on 21 August 1979. *David Rapson*

Below: BR introduced the daytime 'Clansman' service between London Euston and Inverness after the Anglo-Scottish section of the West Coast main line was electrified in 1974. No 47 612 passes Murthly Crossing 'box with the down 'Clansman', the 09.30 departure from Euston, on 20 July 1984. The locomotive had only recently been fitted with electric heating supply and renumbered from 47 080; it had previously been named *Titan* and would have new nameplates fitted by the end of the year. *Paul Shannon*

Secondary and suburban lines

As BR's corporate image became established the secondary and suburban network was still reeling from the effects of the 1963 Beeching report. A significant mileage of rural railway was lost each year up to and including 1970, when BR closed most of the remaining network in East Lincolnshire and various branches elsewhere such as Barnstaple–Ilfracombe, Cambridge–St Ives and Lowestoft–Yarmouth.

On rural routes that survived the axe money for investment was in short supply and facilities tended simply to be downgraded rather than modernised. Dozens of rural stations became unstaffed halts as BR introduced 'Paytrain' operation from the late 1960s onwards. Track layouts were simplified and signalboxes were closed; some branch lines were reduced to the status of a long siding with no run-round facility for locomotive-hauled trains.

The pace of rural line closures slowed considerably after 1970. Local people mounted opposition to closure proposals with increasing success, and BR itself realised that the financial savings gained from closures were often small. Greater savings were to be made by making better use of resources on main lines. Nevertheless, the rural network was not sacrosanct. The year 1972 brought the demise of BR passenger services to Keswick, Swanage, Bridport, Okehampton and Kingswear. Not that the closure was always final: the Kingswear branch passed directly into private hands and became the Torbay Steam Railway, and Swanage and Okehampton have also been revived as heritage railway sites.

In 1973 BR closed the 'Watercress Line' between Alton and Winchester, an island of diesel operation amid the largely electrified Southern Region network. This was another route destined for partial reopening by the preservation movement. Elsewhere on the Southern Region the Ashford–Hastings line had its closure threat lifted thanks to cost-cutting measures such as replacing staffed level crossings with automatic lifting barriers and reducing part of the route to a single track.

In 1975 the Bridport branch in Dorset finally succumbed, having been given a life extension while improvements were made to the local road network. Similar circumstances delayed the closure of the Alston branch in Cumbria until May 1976. On the other hand, the 53½-mile Cambrian Coast line from Dovey Junction to Pwllheli was saved from the threat that had hung over it since 1971 — even though its future would be placed in doubt again when a marine worm infestation was discovered in Barmouth Bridge — and the 63½ miles of single track from Dingwall to Kyle of Lochalsh was also given a welcome reprieve.

Many rural lines had survived beyond the Beeching era thanks to the use of diesel multiple-units, introduced from the late 1950s. A few DMU types, such as the Park Royal Class 103s and the Gloucester Class 100s, were targets for early withdrawal, but the majority of the fleet remained in use well into the 1980s. Their eventual replacement was foreshadowed by two contrasting prototypes, both of which appeared in 1981 — the cheap-and-cheerful Class 140 Leyland railbus and the rather more up-market Class 210 diesel-electric unit.

Despite the proven cost-effectiveness of DMUs, a number of rural lines reverted to locomotive-hauled operation in the 1970s and 1980s as their DMUs became life-expired and as serviceable Mk 1 coaching stock was displaced from Inter-City lines. The change affected mainly longer-distance cross-country routes such as Portsmouth–Cardiff, Norwich–Birmingham and Manchester– Cleethorpes. In later years many of the trains were hauled by Class 31s, newly equipped to supply electric train heating, but other locomotive classes also saw increased passenger use, notably the Class 33s, which ventured as far as West Wales, Manchester and North Wales. The locomotives and stock generally gave way to second-generation 'Sprinter' DMUs as soon as these became available.

In London and the South East BR maintained its complex network of commuter services, but traffic declined steadily in the 1970s, and major investment schemes were relatively few. On the Southern Region little significant change took place other than the replacement of life-expired rolling stock, such as the '4-SUB' units whose design dated back to Southern Railway days. In their place came the four-car Class 508 units, based on the prototype high-density '4-PEP' stock that BR had introduced in 1971. Leaving aside the underground Waterloo & City line, the Class 508 units were the first production build of Southern Region EMU stock to have sliding doors. For longer distance services on third-rail territory, the delivery of '4-CIG' and '4-VEP' units continued into the 1970s, by which time their Mk 1 carriage design was very much yesterday's technology. The first major electrification scheme to be carried out on the Southern Region for many years, from Tonbridge to Hastings, was finally authorised in 1983.

North of the Thames the commuter network developed at different rates on different lines. Out of Paddington and Marylebone the service patterns and diesel rolling stock established in the 1960s continued into the 1980s. Incredible though it seems today, Marylebone was proposed for closure in the early 1980s, with BR planning to divert High

Wycombe trains to Paddington and reduce the service on the Amersham line to a shuttle between Aylesbury and Amersham. Marylebone itself would have become a bus station.

Out of Euston BR continued to operate DC third-rail electric services to Watford Junction and AC overhead services to Bletchley and beyond. The Class 501 DC units would be replaced in the 1980s by Class 313s displaced from the Eastern Region; the '313s' would also operate in overhead mode on the St Albans Abbey branch after its electrification in 1988. A crucial first step in developing the North London line was the reopening of the Dalston–Stratford line for a new Camden Road–North Woolwich service in 1979; however, this was also the beginning of the end for Broad Street, which was to lose its all-day Richmond service in 1985 and close completely the following year.

Commuter services out of St Pancras were transformed by the Bedford-line electrification scheme, completed in 1983. Not only did this mean new, faster trains and a new passenger station for Bedford, but also a doubling of the off-peak service frequency between London and Luton from two to four trains an hour. The Moorgate branch gained an all-day service in place of the previous handful of peak-hour trains.

The former Great Northern lines out of King's Cross also benefited from total route modernisation. Electrification reached Welwyn Garden City and Hertford in 1976 and Royston in 1978. The first stage of the scheme saw the retirement of the last suburban hauled compartment stock on BR, as well as the closure of the King's Cross 'widened lines' which had carried peak-hour trains to Moorgate. All daytime GN inner suburban services now ran to Moorgate via the Northern City line. Once electrification had reached Royston, BR withdrew its through loco-hauled service between King's Cross and Cambridge, the celebrated 'Cambridge Buffet Express'.

Suburban services from Liverpool Street and Fenchurch Street continued to rely mainly on EMU stock built in the late 1950s and early 1960s. One notable exception was the fleet of LNER-design Class 306 units operating on the Shenfield line, which dated back to 1949. These were finally replaced in the early 1980s by sliding-door Class 315 stock, similar in design to the Southern Region Class 508s and Great Northern '313s'.

Outside London responsibility for local train services in Britain's largest urban areas fell to the newly created Passenger Transport Executives (PTEs). Between 1969 and 1974 PTEs were established for the West Midlands, Greater Manchester (originally SELNEC — South East Lancashire, North East Cheshire), Merseyside, Tyne & Wear (originally Tyneside), Greater Glasgow (later renamed Strathclyde), South Yorkshire and West Yorkshire. Although there would continue to be occasional closures — the Kilmacolm branch in Strathclyde and the Clayton West branch in West Yorkshire both closed in 1983 — the PTEs were generally keen to support rail and invest in service improvements. Ownership of the trains and infrastructure remained with BR.

West Midlands PTE upgraded its network by launching a new intensive service between Four Oaks and Longbridge on the Cross City line in 1978, including several new or rebuilt stations. That service was later extended to Redditch — once a rural branch line earmarked for closure — and further enhanced by electrification.

In Greater Manchester early plans for a 'Picc-Vic' tunnel to carry trains under the city centre were abandoned on grounds of cost, but the PTE provided a new passenger terminus for Bury in 1980 and continued to support the Oldham–Rochdale line, which had narrowly escaped closure. The Greater Manchester network included some interesting non-standard electrification systems: the 1,500V DC overhead supply on the Altrincham line was switched to 25kV AC in 1971, and the 1,500V DC system on the Manchester–Glossop/Hadfield line similarly converted in 1984, while the Bury line would retain its unique side-contact 1,200V DC third-rail electrification until conversion to Metrolink in 1991/2. On non-electrified lines Greater Manchester was the first PTE area to receive an allocation of Class 142 railbuses, their bright orange livery representing a decisive break from BR blue.

Merseyside benefited from substantial rail investment in the 1970s with the building of the underground 'link' and 'loop' lines in Liverpool city centre — a project which involved the closure of the run-down Exchange terminus as well as extensions of the DC electrified network to Kirkby and Garston. The Garston line had previously lost its passenger trains when BR withdrew the Liverpool Central–Gateacre service in 1972. As for rolling stock, the LMS-design 650V DC Class 502 and Class 503 EMUs used on the Merseyside network were replaced between 1978 and 1985 by Class 507 and Class 508 stock.

On Tyneside the focus for rail investment was the building of the Tyne & Wear Metro, which between 1980 and 1983 took over the former BR lines to South Shields, Bank Foot and the Tynemouth loop.

Greater Glasgow PTE inherited the largest network of commuter lines in the UK outside London. The city's rail system was boosted in 1979 by the reopening of the Argyle line from Partick to Rutherglen via Glasgow Central Low Level, providing the first electrified link between the north and south networks. Sixteen new Class 314 EMUs were provided for the Argyle line, supplementing the Class 303 and Class 311 'Blue Trains' that had been introduced in the 1960s.

In West and South Yorkshire the PTEs began a programme of opening new stations on existing local lines, among the first examples being Saltaire, Crossflatts, Deighton, Slaithwaite, Bramley and Fitzwilliam. In South Yorkshire the long-mooted closure of the Penistone–Sheffield line to passengers was allowed to proceed, but in its place trains were restored to the Penistone–Barnsley line. Meanwhile some first-generation DMUs in West Yorkshire gave way in 1984 to Class 141 railbuses — a change that was not universally welcomed!

Above: With parcels accommodation comprising a vintage Great Western-design 'Siphon G' flanked by two BR gangwayed brake (BG) vans, Class 35 'Hymek' No 7045 passes Fairwood Junction on the approach to Westbury with the 09.52 Weymouth–Bristol on 19 August 1972. *Hugh Ballantyne*

Below: Class 33-hauled trains formed welcome replacements for DMUs on the Bristol– Portsmouth route. No 33 021 passes Hawkeridge Junction on the outskirts of Westbury with the 10.14 service from Bristol Temple Meads on 29 July 1982. No 33 021 was to retire from the main line in 1996 but would later be reinstated as a member of the Fragonset fleet. At the time of writing it is owned by Nemesis Rail and based at Tyseley. *Paul Shannon*

Left: Pressed Steel Class 117 DMUs worked suburban trains out of London Paddington from 1960 until the arrival of the second-generation 'Networker Turbo' units in 1992. Cars W51349, W59501 and W51391 pass Old Oak Common on an Oxford-bound working on 6 April 1978. *Paul Shannon*

Below left: Following the Beeching closures the last remaining railway line on the Isle of Wight, from Ryde to Shanklin, was electrified. Steam was replaced by a small fleet of former London Underground rolling stock dating back to the 1920s. Class 486 '3-TIS' unit No 034 stands at Ryde Pier Head on the shuttle service to Ryde Esplanade on 6 July 1976. *Paul Shannon*

Below: The two prototype Class 210 diesel-electric multiple-units built in 1981 operated successfully on suburban services out of Paddington, but the design proved too costly, and no bulk order for the type was placed. No 210 002 passes Acton Yard as the 13.05 Paddington–Slough 'stopper' on 8 August 1983. *Paul Shannon*

Above right: A number of '2-HAP' units had their First-class accommodation downgraded to Second and were re-designated '2-SAP' (Class 418) for use on suburban services. '2-SAP' units Nos 5928 and 5935 pass under Clapham Junction 'A' signalbox with a Hounslow-loop service on 6 June 1979. *Paul Shannon*

Right: The '4-SUB' EMU was a highly successful design, developed by the Southern Railway before World War 2. Known latterly as Class 405s, many examples survived into the early 1980s. Unit 4754 waits at the rather bleak Epsom Downs terminus on 21 September 1981 before returning on the half-hourly all-stations service to Victoria. In the distance is the 1879-built Epsom Downs signalbox, which was due to close in 1982 with the opening of Victoria Signalling Centre but was actually destroyed by fire just a few weeks after the date of this photograph. *Paul Shannon*

Above: The Southern Region's diesel-electric multiple units were divided between Eastleigh and St Leonards depots. Carrying the SE code for St Leonards, '3-D' unit No 1311 is pictured at Eridge station on 22 May 1981. Eridge would lose its junction status when the line to Tunbridge Wells closed in 1985. *Hugh Ballantyne*

Below: Converted in the 1970s from a pair of redundant '4-SUB' motor coaches, Class 930 de-icing and Sandite unit No 003 approaches Horsham on 24 December 1991. By this time all-over blue livery was long extinct on passenger-carrying EMUs, and even the later BR blue-and-grey was becoming rare. *Paul Shannon*

Above: Class 501 cars M61153, M70153 and M75153 rattle over the pointwork on arrival at Watford Junction on an evening service from Croxley Green on 16 April 1981. The Class 501 units were to remain in use until replaced in 1985 by dual-voltage Class 313 units from the Eastern Region, while the Croxley Green branch would last until 1996, albeit enjoying only a token service in its later years. *Paul Shannon*

Below: Although suburban services out of St Pancras were worked by Class 127 diesel-hydraulic units, peak-hour trains from Moorgate used Class 116 stock, with an extra power car attached because of the incline between Farringdon and Kentish Town. Cars M50060, M59348, M50893 and M50111 head north between St Albans and Harpenden on a Moorgate–Luton working on 18 September 1978. *Paul Shannon*

Left: The 10 Class 23 'Baby Deltics' spent their short lives working mainly outer-suburban passenger services out of King's Cross. Just one example, No D5909, received Rail-blue livery, being seen so adorned at Hitchin diesel depot in June 1969. *Geoff Plumb collection*

Below left: No 31 129 was one of the last members of its class to be built with folding discs rather than roof-mounted headcode panels. It is pictured calls at Tottenham Hale with one of the two-hourly semi-fast trains to Cambridge on 6 June 1979. *Paul Shannon*

Below: Passing the unusual Stratford Southern signalbox, which originally had a siding directly beneath it, Class 105 cars E53365 and E54126 pull away from Stratford's low-level platforms while working the 11.58 Camden Road–North Woolwich service on 18 February 1985. The railway here was subsequently resignalled and electrified, while the top half of the signalbox was preserved for eventual reinstallation at Dereham, on the Mid-Norfolk Railway. The North Woolwich branch closed in 2006, its function to be served by an extension of the Docklands Light Railway. *Paul Shannon*

Above right: In the late 1960s some Gloucester Class 100 two-car DMUs were transferred from Scotland to East Anglia, working from Norwich and Cambridge depots. A Class 100 set leaves Brundall on a Norwich–Yarmouth service via Acle on 26 May 1977. *Hugh Ballantyne*

Right: Three batches of Class 312 units were built in the 1970s for Great Northern, Great Eastern and London Midland Region outer-suburban services. Visually similar to the Class 310 units of the 1960s, the '312s' were the last new build of slam-door electric stock on BR. Pictured between the tunnels at Welwyn North on 4 April 1980 is unit No 312 724 on a Royston–King's Cross working. *Paul Shannon*

Above: The Skegness line was well known for its locomotive-hauled holiday and excursion trains, which often brought freight locomotives to the Lincolnshire coast. Tinsley-allocated 'Peak' No 45 017 catches the last of the day's sunshine as it passes Ancaster with the 07.35 from Sheffield to Skegness on 1 August 1981. *Paul Shannon*

Below: Pairs of normally freight-only Class 20s continued to power the 'Jolly Fisherman' excursion trains to Skegness in the 1980s, making the Lincolnshire resort a popular destination for enthusiasts. Nos 20 128 and 20 144 await departure with the 11.58 return service to Leicester on 11 August 1984. *David Rapson*

Above: Originally designated Inter-City stock, the Swindon Class 123 units were the last batch of first-generation DMU vehicles supplied to BR. They spent the first part of their lives on the Western Region but were transferred north in the late 1970s to work trans-Pennine services. A four-car Class 123 formation heads west near Kildwick as the 17.12 Leeds–Morecambe train on 21 July 1982. *Paul Shannon*

Below: The Class 124 'Trans-Pennine' DMUs originally ran in six-car formations, each with four powered vehicles in order to tackle the Pennine gradients, but by the late 1970s the buffet cars had been scrapped and four-car formations were standard. Motor Composite No E51967 leads a four-car set past Totley Tunnel East 'box on 5 July 1983, forming the 08.45 from Manchester Piccadilly to Cleethorpes. Less than a year later the entire Class 124 fleet would be withdrawn. *Paul Shannon*

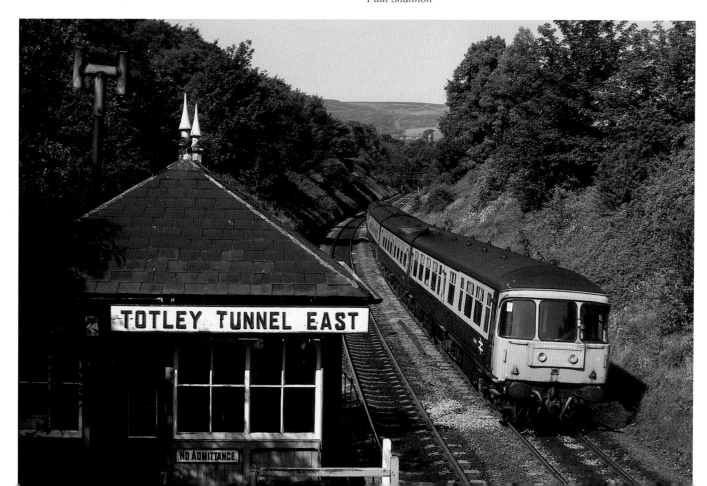

Above: The Derby Class 114 units were the first DMUs ordered under the 1955 Modernisation Plan. They were allocated initially to Lincoln and remained based there for many years. Cars E50026 and E56013 pass Lincoln coal concentration depot with a train for Cleethorpes on 23 August 1978. *Paul Shannon*

Below: Gilberdyke Junction signalbox, opened by the North Eastern Railway in 1903, provides the setting for No 31 430 as it heads east with the 12.19 Leeds–Hull on 25 July 1984. At this time Class 31s were frequent performers on semi-fast trains to Hull, some services starting from Manchester and others from Lancaster. *Paul Shannon*

Above: Taking a break from its usual freight duties, No 47 329 comes off the Lincoln line at Wrawby Junction, Barnetby, with a day excursion train from Burton-upon-Trent to Cleethorpes on 1 August 1984. This locomotive was later to be rebuilt as No 57 011, working initially for Freightliner and later for Direct Rail Services. *Paul Shannon*

Below: Class 03 shunters worked as station pilots at various Eastern Region locations. They were normally coupled to match wagons because the wheelbase of the locomotive was too short to be relied upon to activate some track circuits. No 2113 scurries around Scarborough station on 21 April 1973. *David Rapson*

Above: No 25 219 passes under the unusual suspension footbridge at Whitchurch with train 2V67, the 10.00 from Crewe to Cardiff, on 22 June 1977. Class 25s had then only recently taken over this route from 'Cross-Country' DMUs. *David Rapson*

Left: The Alston branch was earmarked for closure in the 1963 Beeching report but actually survived until 1976. In its later years it was worked as a long siding from Haltwhistle, with its stations unstaffed. Class 108 two-car set Nos E56195 and E50620 stands at the forlorn Alston terminus on 20 March 1976. *Paul Shannon*

Below: Although some depots kept DMUs in semi-permanently coupled sets, others treated their fleets as individual cars which could be re-formed into sets as necessary. This often produced combinations of different liveries. Class 101 cars E56387 and E51225 stand at Alnmouth ready to depart with an early-afternoon stopping train to Newcastle on 12 August 1981. *Paul Shannon*

Above: In their later years the Class 40s appeared more on secondary passenger trains than on front-line expresses, while also retaining their freight and parcels duties. 'Whistler' No 40 110 heads south from Helsby with train 2D62, the 09.33 from Manchester Victoria to Llandudno, on 23 August 1976. *David Rapson*

Below: The sight of a blue Class 47 on blue-and-grey Mk 1 coaching stock was once dismissed as commonplace but would eventually be consigned to history as new liveries swept away the BR corporate image and as locomotive-hauled trains gave way to multiple-units. No 47 452 passes Abergele with the 08.15 from Holyhead to Crewe on 14 August 1982. *Paul Shannon*

Above: Although the Woodhead route lost its through passenger trains in 1970, the suburban service from Manchester to Glossop and Hadfield continued to use 1950s-vintage 1,500V DC EMUs until 1984. A three-car Class 506 set crosses Dinting Viaduct on 12 October 1974. *David Rapson*

Below: One of the unique Class 504 DC electric units with side-contact current collection, comprising cars M65460 and M77171, heads into Heaton Park Tunnel while working the 15.00 Bury–Manchester Victoria service on 16 May 1977. These units would remain in use until the line closed for conversion to Metrolink in 1991. *David Rapson*

Above: Having originally been electrified at 1,500V DC, the Manchester–Altrincham line was converted in 1971 to 25kV AC, enabling through operation between Altrincham and Crewe. Class 304 unit No 043 calls at Timperley on an Altrincham-bound service on 25 October 1982. Ten years later the electrification system was to change again upon conversion of the line to Metrolink operation at 750V DC. *Paul Shannon*

Below: Forming the 16.39 Blackburn–Manchester Victoria service, Class 104 cars M53443 and M53493 pass the Lancashire & Yorkshire Railway signalbox at Bromley Cross on 6 June 1983. Today the semaphore signal has been replaced by a colour light, but the signalbox survives as an interface between the incompatible train-describers of Preston and Manchester Piccadilly power 'boxes. *Paul Shannon*

Above left: In the summer of 1992 BR introduced double-headed Class 31s on peak-hour trains between Manchester and Blackpool. With Regional Railways-liveried early Mk 2 stock in tow Nos 31 432 and 31 442 leave Bolton with the 07.06 from Blackpool North on 6 July 1992. On the right is an early example of the palisade fencing which was to ruin many photographic vantage-points in the 21st century. *Paul Shannon*

Left: Rising some 2,273ft above sea level, Pen-y-Ghent provides the backdrop for this view of No 47 451 passing Selside with the 16.07 Leeds–Carlisle on 17 August 1985. The appearance of a Class 47 was disappointing for photographers, given that many trains on the Settle–Carlisle line were Class 31-hauled at this time. *Paul Shannon*

Above: In a bold departure from BR's corporate image, rolling stock used to connect with Stranraer–Larne ferries on both sides of the Irish Sea was painted in Sealink livery. The stock also covered some short workings between Glasgow and Ayr. No 47 537 *Sir Gwynedd / County of Gwynedd* passes Lochside with the 17.12 Glasgow Central–Ayr on 18 July 1984. *Paul Shannon*

Below: The Glasgow & South Western route between Carlisle and Glasgow was downgraded in the BR era, some sections being reduced to single track. No 47 435 regains the double-track section at Barrhead with the 06.00 Carlisle–Glasgow Central train on 15 July 1988, about to pick up some modest commuter traffic for the final stage of its journey. *Paul Shannon*

Above: Class 27 locomotives were the staple traction on the West Highland from dieselisation in the mid-1960s until the arrival of Class 37s in 1981. No 27 033 calls at the idyllic Banavie Halt with the 16.40 from Fort William to Mallaig on 28 June 1975. *David Rapson*

Below: The Great North of Scotland Railway branches to Fraserburgh and Peterhead lost their passenger services in 1965, and Peterhead closed to all traffic in 1970. Class 26 No D5307 pauses at the disused station of Ellon with a special working to mark the demise of the Peterhead branch on 5 September 1970. *Derek Cross*

Above: In an attempt to overcome major technical problems BR had twenty Class 21 diesels re-engined with Paxman 'Ventura' power units to become Class 29. Painted blue but still carrying its steam-age 'D' prefix, Class 29 No D6119 stands at Oban with a Glasgow-bound train on 21 August 1968. The re-engined locomotives were to enjoy a slightly longer lifespan than the unconverted Class 21s, but all would be withdrawn by the end of 1971. *Geoff Plumb collection*

Below: No 26 045 waits at Georgemas Junction with the Wick portion of the late-morning train from Thurso and Wick to Inverness on 5 September 1979. The dual sealed-beam headlights were a feature of Inverness Class 26s at this time. No 26 045 would be withdrawn in July 1983 and later sent to Vic Berry, Leicester, for scrapping. *Paul Shannon*

Mail and parcels

At the start of the Rail-blue period BR still operated a complex network of van trains carrying parcels, mail and newspapers, not to mention occasional trainloads of pigeons! A number of cities had dedicated parcels stations, such as Birmingham Curzon Street, Bricklayers Arms (South London), Manchester Mayfield and Glasgow Salkeld Street. However, the bulk of the traffic was handled at normal passenger stations, many of which became a hive of activity in the late evening and early hours of the morning as passengers gave way to trolley-loads of packages large and small.

Dozens of small stations, serving communities as diverse as Scunthorpe, Skegness and Slough, had one or more sidings where vans were left for unloading and loading during the day. At countless further locations staff would unload and load traffic while the train waited. The combination of detaching or attaching vans at some stations and making extended stops at others could make for slow progress: in Cornwall, for example, the first van train of the day took three hours to cover the 80 miles from Plymouth to Penzance.

Many normal passenger trains also carried various combinations of parcels, mail and newspaper traffic. In a few districts, such as the Far North of Scotland, some passenger trains included a greater number of parcels vans than passenger coaches. Newspaper traffic was by its nature one-way and more time-sensitive than the general parcels business; newspapers tended therefore to be conveyed in dedicated trains. The empty newspaper vans would return to the appropriate carriage sidings, such as Red Bank for Manchester Victoria traffic, during the daytime.

Van trains used a remarkably diverse fleet of rolling stock. Many vehicles built to pre-Nationalisation designs were still in daily use throughout the 1970s. Even at the close of that decade BR retained more than 700 SR-design four-wheeled vans, over 100 SR-design bogie vans, over 300 LMS-design bogie vans and 22 GWR-design 'Siphon G' bogie vans. Most of the Siphon G vehicles were allocated to Western Region newspaper traffic, but the SR- and LMS-design vans could be found throughout the network; for example an SR-design van was regularly included in a West Highland-line passenger working in 1981.

The BR standard design van fleet consisted of over 1,000 bogie gangwayed brake vehicles (BG), many of which ran in passenger train formations, as well as over 500 bogie General Utility Vans (GUV) and over 800 four-wheeled Covered Carriage Trucks (CCT). Some CCT vehicles were painted in 'Tartan Arrow' livery for use on the overnight express freight service between Kentish Town and Glasgow, which finished in the 1970s. The BR van fleet also included more than 70 four-wheeled former fish vans, re-coded SPV, which were to end their working lives on Post Office and Readers Digest traffic from Aylesbury.

Mail traffic included the celebrated Travelling Post Office services, allowing letters to be sorted on the move. These services operated on many lines out of London and on some cross-country routes. They used a dedicated fleet of more than 100 vans, built in the late 1950s and early 1960s to replace older, life-expired stock. Some examples were to remain in use until Royal Mail stopped using rail in 2004. The Travelling Post Office vans wore blue-and-grey livery until 1986, when Parcels Sector red made its appearance.

Although most parcels, mail and newspaper traffic was carried in locomotive-hauled trains, BR had followed the example of the GWR in acquiring a small fleet of self-powered diesel parcels cars. Allocated to the Western and London Midland regions, they had cabs at each end and could operate singly, but often worked in pairs and/or with 'tail traffic' of one or more vans. Passenger-carrying DMUs could also haul parcels vans when required. Of the purpose-built diesel parcels cars, the Cravens design, which numbered only three vehicles, became extinct in the 1970s, but some Gloucester Class 128 units were to survive into the early 1990s. By that time BR had also converted some passenger-carrying DMUs and EMUs to carry parcels or newspapers, although this usage was short-lived.

In terms of the locations served, the parcels network contracted steadily throughout the BR-blue period. The general Rail Express Parcels service, with collection and delivery provided by BR, was withdrawn in 1981, leading to large-scale withdrawals of older rolling stock. The two-axle vans and the surviving pre-Nationalisation types were the first to go, followed by large numbers of BR standard bogie vehicles as the contraction continued. With the benefit of hindsight it is no surprise that parcels traffic would eventually cease altogether. The problem was the high cost of maintaining terminals and rolling stock, combined with the need to shunt small numbers of vans at a large number of locations — very much the same story as wagonload freight.

Right: Rail blue and steam overlapped by a few years, yet pictures featuring both are rare. One of the first Class 40s to embrace BR's new corporate image, No D275, awaits departure from Heysham with a pigeon special to Hereford on 24 May 1968. On the adjacent track is 'Black Five' No 44897 with a ballast train. *Derek Cross*

Below: Mail, parcels and newspaper traffic kept many major passenger stations alive throughout the night. No 74 008, one of the Class 74 electro-diesels that had been converted in 1967/8 from Class 71 electrics, waits to depart London Waterloo with train 6K21, the 03.25 to Richmond, on 2 September 1977. *David Rapson*

Left: A headcode beginning with '3' denoted an express parcels train permitted to run at 90mph or more. Class 85 No 85 034 hurries south near Shap with train 3A65 from Carlisle to London on 4 July 1974. *Derek Cross*

Below: Although based north of the border the Class 27s were frequent visitors to Carlisle. No 27 029 waits to head north from Carlisle Citadel with train 6S17, the 13.23 from Crewe to Glasgow, on 18 July 1978. *David Rapson*

Right: Parcels and mail traffic provided work for Class 08 shunters at many large passenger stations around the network. No 08 951 shunts a goods brake van and a General Utility Van (GUV) at Bristol Temple Meads on 30 July 1987. At this date more than 300 GUV vehicles remained in service, but withdrawals were gathering pace as the parcels network contracted. *Paul Shannon*

Below right: Coded 1M41, the overnight mail train between York and Shrewsbury was a long-standing fixture in the BR timetable. No 45 019 waits to depart from York with train 1M41 on 1 October 1981. *Brian Roberts*

Left: No 37 218 was allocated to the Railfreight Sector while based at Stratford depot but continued to appear on parcels and passenger trains, being pictured passing Stratford station with train 1V66, the 17.59 Southend–Reading vans, on 13 July 1989. The locomotive was to be stored unserviceable in 1995 but would later return to front-line use with Direct Rail Services. *Paul Shannon*

Below left: BR struggled to retain its share of parcels and mail traffic and concentrated increasingly on the premium end of the business, running shorter trains on a reduced number of key routes. No 47 476 passes Hadley Wood with train 1S37, the 19.18 from King's Cross to Aberdeen, on 3 July 1989. *Paul Shannon*

Right: A visit to Wrexham General station on 7 July 1977 found No 24 082 detaching two parcels vans (including ex-LMS BG No M31927, built at Wolverton in 1944) from train 4D29, the 12.15 Shrewsbury–Chester; the two diesel parcels units just visible beyond the footbridge would continue with the third van to Chester. On the platform are a number of British Railways Utility Trolley Equipment (BRUTE) trolleys — an essential feature of parcels operations in the Rail-blue period. *David Rapson*

Below: Parcels vans of LMS, GWR, BR and SR designs make up the load for No 40 133 as it passes Whitchurch on 22 June 1977, the combination running as train 4H15, the 09.50 from Shrewsbury Abbey Foregate to Manchester Mayfield. *David Rapson*

Above: No 86 206 *City of Stoke on Trent* pauses at Hemel Hempstead with an up train of newspaper and parcels vans on 20 September 1979. Just visible on the right is a rake of goods vans which would also have been used for parcels traffic. Although a number of Class 86/2 locomotives are still extant today, No 86 206 was withdrawn in 2002 and later scrapped. *Paul Shannon*

Below: A mixture of old and new at Thirsk: the North Eastern Railway warning sign contrasts with the multiple-aspect signalling as No 31 441 heads south with train 5D40, the 14.55 Heaton–Doncaster empty vans, on 19 August 1988. The masts had recently been installed ready for electrification, which would be energised as far as Northallerton in 1990. *Paul Shannon*

PUBLIC WARNING
PERSONS ARE WARNED NOT TO TRESPASS
ON THIS RAILWAY, OR ON ANY OF THE
LINES, STATIONS, WORKS, OR PREMISES
CONNECTED THEREWITH
ANY PERSON SO TRESPASSING IS LIABLE
TO A PENALTY

Freight in bulk

The start of the Rail-blue period coincided with the birth of bulk trainload freight as we know it today. Faced with the falling costs of road haulage and the shorter journey times made possible by new motorways and trunk roads, BR in the 1960s realised that its best prospects were in the heavy freight sector, where a single locomotive and traincrew could do the job of a small fleet of lorries. Ideally a trainload of freight would move directly between the private sidings of two customers, cutting out the need for road collection or delivery. And in many cases the wagons would be owned or hired by one of the customers, so that BR could avoid the costs and risks of maintaining a large common-user wagon fleet. The role of BR was to provide traction, traincrew and a path on the main line.

In reality it took a long time to reap the full benefits of trainload operation. Often private sidings were not long enough to accommodate a whole train, or traffic volumes were not constant enough to justify a regular service. Nevertheless, by the mid-1970s BR was steadily increasing the typical payload of a block freight train and was ironing out some of the operational complexities that could add time as well as cost to a freight flow.

A welcome boost to rail freight was the Government grant scheme set up through Section 8 of the Transport Act 1974, which provided up to 60% of the funding for new and improved rail freight terminals provided that some environmental benefit could be shown. The grants were later extended to cover rolling stock. Some of the schemes supported by Section 8 funding turned out to be short-lived, but others, such as several flows of stone from Mountsorrel quarry, are still operating at the time of writing.

Few railway innovations can rival the simplicity and effectiveness of the merry-go-round (MGR) coal train, which BR developed in the mid-1960s in conjunction with the Central Electricity Generating Board and the National Coal Board (NCB). By the middle of 1971 some 18 power stations had been equipped to discharge coal from MGR trains on the move, cutting out the need for exchange sidings and shunting locomotives as well as achieving a huge reduction in the wagon fleet. A blue Class 47 or Class 56 locomotive coupled to a rake of 40 or so MGR wagons symbolised rail freight in the 1970s in much the same way as the IC125 came to symbolise high-speed passenger services.

Coal traffic generally lent itself to trainload working as consumers tended to require high-volume deliveries. The MGR concept was applied to almost all power stations as well as to NCB export terminals (in the days when we exported rather than imported coal!), to steelworks such as Scunthorpe, Redcar and Ravenscraig, and to cement works such as Northfleet, Aberthaw and Tring. Between 1965 and 1982 BR acquired a fleet of more than 11,000 MGR hopper wagons — a small figure compared with the hundreds of thousands of old-fashioned mineral wagons and hoppers that they replaced but nevertheless a far bigger fleet than any other wagon type built in the Rail-blue era.

Whilst many 1960s MGR wagons were to remain in front-line service into the 21st century the network of coal trains changed out of all recognition as the British coal industry shrank towards — but not quite reaching — oblivion. When the first blue-liveried locomotives appeared there were well over 400 deep mines in the UK, as well as many opencast sites and blending locations. By the early 1980s that figure had fallen to just over 200 — and that was before the year-long miners' strike, which would give greater impetus to the closure programme.

In contrast to coal, which had always been a staple traffic for the railways, petroleum products were a relatively new source of business in the Rail-blue era. The tonnage of petrol, diesel, heating oil and other refined products moved by rail shot up from 5.2 million tonnes in 1962 to 21.6 million tonnes in 1972. Much of this traffic was conveyed in block trains of 1,000 tonnes or more. The capital investment was almost entirely in the hands of private companies, which provided not only loading racks at the refineries and a network of specialised distribution terminals but also a vast fleet of tank wagons. From the late 1960s new wagon builds were mostly 100-tonne bogie tanks, but many flows would continue to use two-axle vehicles. Unfortunately the investment in rail did not always secure long-term business: some major flows were lost to pipelines and road transport from the late 1970s onwards.

Aggregates traffic was a major success story for the railways in the corporate blue period. As with petroleum, the tonnages of stone, gravel and sand moved by rail increased dramatically as BR signed new contracts with quarrying firms and distributors. In just five years, from 1969 to 1974, that business rose from 2 million tonnes to almost 10 million tonnes — a faster rate of growth than Dr Beeching had dared to predict when he wrote of opportunities for bulk trainload traffic.

The new aggregates flows were concentrated on particular regions and routes. Much of the traffic was destined for London and the South East, where local sources of gravel were quickly becoming exhausted but where large road-building and redevelopment projects were under way. BR picked up some relatively short-distance business, such as sea-dredged aggregates from the Thames estuary to the London area, but the biggest opportunities involved bringing limestone from the Mendips and granite from Leicestershire to numerous terminals spread across the South East.

The Mendips traffic started in 1970 when Foster Yeoman opened a new loading facility at Merehead; this traffic grew so rapidly that BR had to use redundant coal hopper wagons as a stopgap until Foster Yeoman had acquired its own stock. By the early 1980s BR was transporting a total of more than 5 million tonnes of stone from Merehead and its neighbour Whatley. Class 56 locomotives were allocated to the heaviest trains in order to maximise payloads; However, their reliability was an issue and Foster Yeoman soon made the ground-breaking decision to order its own General Motors Class 59s.

The Leicestershire quarries also saw a gradual increase in rail traffic from the 1970s onwards. Major investment went into improving the loading facilities at Mountsorrel and into new fleets of hopper wagons for traffic to the London area and East Anglia, partly funded by Section 8 grants. Mountsorrel was also one of a number of quarries to supply trainloads of railway ballast — regarded as non-revenue traffic in the 1970s, but still very much part of the freight scene.

Further north the railway had fewer opportunities to compete for aggregates traffic, because distances were generally too short. However, several flows of limestone from the Peak District to Manchester and Cheshire were already established, notably the long-standing block trains from Tunstead to Northwich for ICI. BR gradually developed the traffic from Tunstead and from neighbouring Dove Holes, with new air-braked stock coming on stream alongside the elderly ICI hoppers.

Elsewhere, the former Grassington branch in the Yorkshire Dales gained a new lease of life thanks to limestone traffic from the Tilcon quarry at Rylstone. This business provided a good opportunity for intensive diagramming: a single rake of brand-new hopper wagons would make two return journeys each weekday, serving Hull in the morning and Leeds in the evening.

The cement industry gave BR some useful trainload business, with several major firms such as Blue Circle and Castle setting up rail-based distribution terminals. Some high-profile traffic gains in the 1970s included bulk cement trains from the Ribblesdale works at Clitheroe to Middlesbrough, Newcastle and Gunnie, partly funded by a Section 8 grant. Other bulk products that generated trainload volumes at that time were gypsum, lime and flyash.

The steel industry continued to rely on BR for the movement of raw materials, semi-finished and finished products. However, the pattern of rail-borne steel traffic changed fundamentally as the industry itself underwent major restructuring: in 1967 the Iron & Steel Act brought the UK's 14 largest steel companies into public ownership as the British Steel Corporation (BSC), paving the way for some plants to close altogether and others to benefit from selective investment.

One thrust of the programme was to reduce duplication of core activities, especially at the 'heavy' end of steel production. The number of blast furnaces spread across the country shrank from 89 in 1967 to around 20 by the early 1980s, located at the five key sites of Llanwern, Port Talbot, Scunthorpe, Redcar (Teesside) and Ravenscraig. At the same time the BSC switched from using home-produced to imported iron ore. These two factors provided BR with ideal opportunities for heavy trainload operation, intensive services bringing ore from Port Talbot to Llanwern, Immingham to Scunthorpe and Hunterston to Ravenscraig.

The restructuring of BSC also produced some high-volume flows of semi-finished steel, now that different plants were specialising in different stages of the steel-making process. For example, Corby lost its blast furnaces and rolling mill but specialised in manufacturing tubes; it therefore started to receive trainloads of rolled steel coil from Teesside. The former John Summers works at Shotton became a secondary processing plant and began to receive semi-finished coil from Ravenscraig, Llanwern and Port Talbot. The Workington plant would manufacture steel rail from blooms, transported by rail from Teesside and Scunthorpe.

The new flows of semi-finished coil and blooms were prime examples of efficient trainload working. On the Teesside–Corby route each of two daily trains completed its out and back journey in less than 24 hours and conveyed some 60 coils, rising to 80 coils from 1983.

At the finished end of the steel-industry spectrum BR gained numerous flows of cars and vans to and from factories, ports and distribution terminals. Using double-deck Cartic wagons to maximise the use of train space BR launched a daily block train between Halewood and Dagenham, carrying Ford vehicles in both directions. Other notable flows in the 1970s included Dagenham–Elderslie, Dagenham–Wakefield and Longbridge–Bathgate.

Trainload efficiencies were also achieved in the general distribution market thanks to Freightliner, which operation's first revenue-earning container train ran from London to Glasgow on 15 November 1965. Designed originally for domestic rather than deep-sea container traffic, the Freightliner network expanded rapidly and served 17 terminals by May 1968. Soon Freightliner began to shift its emphasis to the deep-sea ports, with new terminals coming on stream at Tilbury, Southampton and Felixstowe. Improvements to terminal layouts and the use of more powerful locomotives enabled Freightliner gradually to lengthen its trains, helping to fend off road competition on its core routes.

The cement works at Hope generated inward coal as well as outward cement traffic, just as it still does at the time of writing. No 47 374 passes Bamford with train 8M65, the 16.46 Dovecliffe–Earles Sidings (Hope) coal, on 4 July 1983. The wagons were vacuum-braked HTV hoppers, of which more than 8,000 examples remained in service at that time. *Paul Shannon*

Above: The Coalville line lost its passenger service in 1964 but remained busy with coal and other freight traffic into the 1980s. Nos 20 157 and 20 140 pass Coalville crossing with empty HUO and MEO coal wagons for Snibston colliery on 5 January 1981. The 1907-built signalbox was later decommissioned but survives today as a visitor attraction at Snibston Discovery Park. *Paul Shannon*

Below: Class 56 locomotives became the staple traction for merry-go-round coal trains on many parts of the BR network. No 56 064 draws forward slowly past Moira West Junction 'box as its train of HAA wagons is loaded at Rawdon colliery on 11 April 1983. The tracks curving around to the right gave access to Overseal sidings, on the rump of the former branch to Donisthorpe and Measham. *Paul Shannon*

Above: Both the locomotive and the wagons were nearing the end of their lives when 'Peak' No 45 015 was photographed passing Alfreton & Mansfield Parkway with an up train of empty MXV mineral wagons on 24 July 1984. At this time Alfreton & Mansfield Parkway station was still relatively new, having opened in 1973. *Paul Shannon*

Below: The rare combination of lying snow and sun produces an attractive scene at Bullhouse, east of Dunford Bridge, as No 76 040 heads west with Yorkshire coal for export to Ireland via Garston on 23 March 1979. Diesel traction would take over at Godley Junction. *Brian Roberts*

Above: Relics of West Cumbria's industrial past frame No 47 292 as it passes Parton with train 7F22, the 08.33 Maryport–Fiddlers Ferry merry-go-round coal working, on 13 July 1983. At this time Fiddlers Ferry took coal from two Cumbrian sources — Maryport opencast disposal point and Haig Colliery. No 47 292 was to survive into the 21st century as a Freightliner locomotive and has since been preserved. *Paul Shannon*

Below: One of the original Romanian-built Class 56s, No 56 007, stabled at Doncaster depot on 28 May 1978. On the left is the former Class 08 shunter No D3078, converted to a snowplough and wearing a hybrid green/blue livery. *Brian Roberts*

Above: One of the last Class 56s to retain blue livery, No 56 022 passes Clay Cross on 28 August 1992 with train 7O34, the 17.43 Oxcroft–Ridham Dock merry-go-round working, with coal destined for the Bowaters paper mill at Sittingbourne. No 56 022 was to remain in service until 1999; it was later purchased by ECT Mainline Rail and moved to the Weardale Railway for storage. *Paul Shannon*

Below: A number of Class 20s finished up working merry-go-round coal trains in the North West while remaining allocated to Toton depot for maintenance. Nos 20 143 and 20 130 negotiate Crosfields Crossing, Warrington, with empty merry-go-round coal hoppers from Fiddlers Ferry on 8 September 1990. *Paul Shannon*

Left: At the start of 1973 a total of 99 Class 37s were allocated to South Wales depots — an indication of the huge volume of coal, steel and other heavy freight that BR was moving at that time. No 6607 stands at Severn Tunnel Junction stabling point on 19 August 1973. This locomotive would become No 37 307 under the TOPS renumbering scheme and would be further renumbered 37 403 when refurbished and fitted with ETH supply in 1984. It survived into the 21st century and at the time of writing is undergoing restoration on the Bo'ness & Kinneil Railway. *David Rapson*

Below left: BR ran up to 15 trainloads of imported iron ore each weekday from Bidston to Shotton for the British Steel Corporation's blast furnaces. The trains comprised bogie hopper wagons similar to those used by ICI on the long-standing limestone traffic from Tunstead, but they were unfitted and trains therefore required a brake van. Nos 25 161 and 25 041 pass Burton Point with train 9F20, the 15.06 departure from Bidston Dock, on 1 July 1976. *David Rapson*

Right: The reshaping of Britain's steel industry in the late 1970s produced new rail-borne flows of semi-finished steel, including the flagship 'Steelliner' service conveying hot rolled coil from Lackenby strip mill to Corby tube works. This service used purpose-built BAA and BBA wagons with corrugated decking to aid the dissipation of heat from the freshly cast coils. Pioneer Class 40 No 40 122 passes Treeton Junction with the Corby-bound train, running as 6Z68, on 23 September 1980. *Paul Shannon*

Below: A classic scene of heavy industry, which provided BR Railfreight with its core business in many parts of the country. With the steelworks formerly owned by John Summers dominating the scene, No 40 176 leaves Dee Marsh Junction sidings with train 6Z31, the 08.00 empty steel working to Llanwern, on 5 September 1979. The sidings contain two ferry vans, several hooded coil carriers of GWR design, and numerous internal wagons owned by the British Steel Corporation. *David Rapson*

Left: Bright steel coils form the load for train 6M47, the 12.05 from Lackenby to Corby, as it passes Monk Fryston behind a pair of Class 31 locomotives on 11 August 1981. One hour's observation at Monk Fryston on that date produced six different locomotive classes — 25, 31, 37, 45, 47 and 56. *Paul Shannon*

Below: The Class 85 electrics retained their corporate blue livery long after most Class 86s had been repainted in business-sector colours. No 85 007 passes Greenholme with train 6S50, the 12.36 Dee Marsh Junction–Mossend empty steel working, on 8 April 1989. The BAA and BBA wagons would be reloaded with slab at Ravenscraig. *Paul Shannon*

Right: The Stirling area was well known for its semaphore signals, including this fine gantry controlled from Stirling Middle 'box, which survived until 1985. No 27 049 heads south on 19 July 1984 with train 7A61, the 11.08 Inverness–Ardrossan Harbour, comprising empty bitumen tanks from Culloden Moor. *Paul Shannon*

Below right: The letter 'G' in the headcode denotes a special working, as Class 37 No 6737 crawls through Doncaster station with southbound bogie tanks on 19 January 1974. Within a few weeks this locomotive would be renumbered 37 037; its later career would include a three-year spell as No 37 321 while working in Scotland and a one-year foray to France for hauling infrastructure trains in 1999/2000, before being purchased for preservation by the Devon Diesel Society. *Brian Roberts*

Above: Ripple Lane East sidings were used as a staging point for block oil trains from the two refineries on the Thames Haven branch. No 47 288 sets out from Ripple Lane with two-axle tanks on 18 February 1985. In the background is Ripple Lane Freightliner terminal, which at that time handled two daily trains to and from Southampton. *Paul Shannon*

Below: Blue No 33 030 is paired with Trainload Construction-liveried locomotive No 33 033 as it heads west on the Great Western main line between Old Oak Common and Acton with 'Seacow' hoppers on 31 October 1988. No 33 033 would later be despatched to the scrapyard, but at the time of writing No 33 030 remains active with West Coast Railways. *Paul Shannon*

Right: Many Class 20s retained their blue livery until withdrawn from BR stock. Nos 20 078 and 20 151 depart Wirksworth yard on 30 October 1989 with HTV hoppers carrying sugar stone for South Lynn. This was a seasonal traffic flow which operated for the last time in 1989/90, leaving the branch from Duffield disused until the Ecclesbourne Valley Railway became established. *Paul Shannon*

Above: In the very early days of a freight operation that was later to expand dramatically, 'Western' No D1058 *Western Nobleman* arrives at Merehead on the then newly built arrival line on 3 September 1976. The train consists of former iron ore tippler wagons, which were allocated to roadstone traffic at that time. *Hugh Ballantyne*

Below: Loaded trains leaving Tunstead quarry often required banking assistance. No 25 212 is the banker for train 6H59 to Portwood as it passes Great Rocks Junction on 25 October 1982, with train engine No 37 092 at the front. This train was one of several roadstone workings which shared the use of ICI's vacuum-braked bogie hopper wagons. *Paul Shannon*

Above: Double-headed Class 33s continued to appear on freight duties in the early 1990s, about half the class being allocated to Trainload Construction and based at Stewarts Lane depot. Nos 33 020 and 33 027 pass the diminutive Charlton Lane Crossing 'box with train 7V78, the 09.12 Angerstein Wharf–Park Royal aggregates, on 2 August 1990. *Paul Shannon*

Below: A fine portrait of 'Western' No D1013 *Western Ranger* preparing to depart Westbury sidings with the 21.25 stone train to Acton on 1 December 1977. Today this locomotive can be seen in action on the Severn Valley Railway. *G. G. Vincent*

Above: Among the more modern wagons used for railway-infrastructure traffic in the 1980s were the YGH 'Sealion' and YGB 'Seacow' ballast hoppers introduced from 1970. No 31 152 approaches Welwyn Garden City with a southbound rake of 'Seacows' on 23 August 1988. *Paul Shannon*

Below: The cement works at Eastgate produced block trains for Grangemouth, Irvine, Heaton and Sunderland, as well as wagonload traffic for other distribution terminals. No 37 078 heads north near Durham with train 6S57, the 07.10 Eastgate–Irvine, on 14 May 1982. This locomotive would be withdrawn from service at the end of 1993 but then faced a long period of storage before being scrapped in 2004. *Paul Shannon*

Above: Most grain traffic moved in small quantities on the wagonload network, but BR also ran block trains to Scottish distilleries via the East Coast main line. No 47 322 passes Elgin with empty grain hoppers — often known as 'whisky wagons' because of the advertising panels carried by some examples — on 25 September 1980. *Paul Shannon*

Below: The Class 83 electrics were among the less successful types built for the electrified West Coast main line. The entire class was stored from 1969 until 1973/4 because of technical problems, and the bulk of the fleet was withdrawn in 1983. No 83 012 survived in service rather longer and is now preserved at Barrow Hill Roundhouse, carrying its original number E3035. Back in BR days, it awaits a crew change at Warrington Bank Quay with train 4E35, the 11.25 Elderslie–Dagenham Dock 'Cartic' wagons, on 16 February 1977. *Brian Roberts*

Left: Having only just received its TOPS identity, No 47 286 passes Potters Bar with southbound 'Cartic' wagons on 16 March 1974. The number '4' in the headcode denoted a freight or parcels train authorised to run at 75mph, while the letter 'C' denoted a destination in the Liverpool Street division, most likely to have been Dagenham for this train. *David Rapson*

Below left: Although moved between Merseyside and Dagenham in block trains, automotive wagons were shunted in and out of Garston car terminal by a Class 08 pilot locomotive, adding to the complexity and cost of the operation. No 08 739 performs this duty on 6 April 1995. *Paul Shannon*

Right: Leeds Freightliner terminal was opened in 1967 and is still one of Freightliner's core regional terminals more than 40 years later. No 47 307 is seen having just arrived at Leeds with train 4D79, the 15.12 feeder service from Immingham, on 8 August 1989. On the adjacent track is pilot locomotive No 08 874. *Paul Shannon*

Below: Just a few weeks after being name *Wilton Endeavour*, No 47 361 passes Eaglescliffe with train 4K75, the 18.05 Stockton–Darlington Freightliner service, on 15 August 1983. This was one of three evening departures from Stockton at the time and included portions for Trafford Park and Cardiff Pengam.
No 47 361 would later become a member of the privatised Freightliner fleet, ultimately being scrapped in 2004. *Paul Shannon*

Above: Container traffic between England and Ireland produced several daily Freightliner trains along the North Wales coast until Freightliner closed its Holyhead terminal in 1991. No 40 166, one of the Class 40s originally based in Scotland but transferred to Longsight in 1978, passes Connah's Quay with train 4G66, the 05.51 from Holyhead to Birmingham Lawley Street, on 14 May 1979. *David Rapson*

Below: Approaching Watford Junction on 16 April 1981 are Nos 86 003 and 86 010 with a northbound Freightliner working. No 86 003 was to end its revenue-earning days in 1999 as No 86 603, while No 86 010 would become No 86 610 and at the time of writing is still in service with Freightliner. *Paul Shannon*

Above: The sole thyristor-controlled Class 87 locomotive, No 87 101 *Stephenson*, was allocated to Railfreight Distribution in contrast to the 35 standard Class 87s, which went to InterCity West Coast. It regained its BR blue livery for its last few years in service. Here it passes Whitmore with train 4A15, the 15.12 Trafford Park–Wembley intermodal, on 30 March 1998. *Paul Shannon*

Below: Although designed as mixed-traffic locomotives, the Sulzer-powered Class 25s were increasingly devoted to freight duties in their later years. Nos 25 214, 25 123 and 25 218 undergo repairs at Derby Works on 10 March 1979. The 'Sulzers' had a long association with Derby Works: many examples were built there, and the class continued to receive classified repairs there until 1981. *Paul Shannon*

Above: From April 1979 until its withdrawal in October 1980 No 24 081 was the only Class 24 locomotive remaining in service. On 21 August 1979 it heads north through Crewe station with failed No 47 480 in tow. Snapped up for preservation, following its eventual withdrawal, No 24 081 is currently one of 15 diesel locomotives based on the Gloucestershire–Warwickshire Railway. *Paul Shannon*

Below: In the heyday of rail-borne petroleum trains loaded services ran in both directions across the Pennines — from the Immingham refineries to depots in the North West and from the Stanlow refinery to depots in Yorkshire and the North East. On 8 July 1983 No 40 152 passes Eastwood with train 7E60, the 10.40 Preston Docks–Lindsey (Immingham) empty tanks. The railway still carries bitumen from Lindsey to Preston Docks at the time of writing, using a new generation of rolling-stock which entered service in 2010. *Paul Shannon*

Wagonload freight

The Rail-blue period saw the beginning of less-than-trainload freight traffic on BR. Already the railway had given up its obligation as common carrier, which had required a comprehensive network of goods stations and delivery services. During the mid-1960s hundreds of stations lost their freight facilities as BR cut back on lightly loaded trip workings and local shunting duties. Wherever possible major freight flows were reorganised to run in full trainloads, while hopelessly uneconomic flows were simply abandoned. Between 1968 and 1972 the proportion of rail freight tonnage moved by the wagonload network declined from 69% to 33%; by 1977 it had fallen further, to 20%.

As wagonload freight traffic ebbed away so BR's network of marshalling yards became an expensive embarrassment. Many of them had been built or rebuilt as mechanised hump yards under the 1955 Modernisation Plan and were therefore relatively new. Some were destined never to handle the throughput that they were designed for. A case in point is Carlisle Kingmoor, which had the capacity to handle 5,000 wagons a day when completed in 1963 but never actually handled more than 4,000 before rapid decline set in. The down sidings at Kingmoor closed in 1973 and all traffic was diverted to the former up sidings; even then there was plenty of spare capacity and by 1981 all hump shunting at Kingmoor had ceased.

Marshalling yards were subject to cutbacks even in heavily industrialised areas. Tees Yard, completed in 1963, never achieved the daily throughput of 7,000 wagons for which it was designed. By 1979 it was handling fewer than 2,000 wagons a day and rationalisation was inevitable. The up hump and reception sidings were closed in 1982, followed by the remaining down hump three years later. Flat shunting was adequate for the traffic that remained.

Nevertheless, a few marshalling yards managed to remain busy throughout the 1970s. The timetable for the adjacent Warrington Arpley and Walton Old Junction yards in 1978 shows a total of 29 trunk wagonload trains scheduled to start, terminate or call there on an average weekday. Direct trains were available to most major centres, stretching from Dundee and Mossend in the North to Exeter, Eastleigh and Dover in the South. The Warrington yards also supported numerous local trip workings, serving locations in the Manchester and Liverpool areas as well as Cheshire and central Lancashire.

Although most stations had lost their public goods facilities by the late 1960s, BR still served hundreds of sidings where wagonload freight could be loaded or unloaded. Even as late as 1981 BR itself operated 74 public freight terminals with cranes for handling steel and other heavy loads. Such terminals could accept a bewildering variety of freight traffic. At Cambridge Coalfields, for example, a survey conducted over seven months in 1979 showed 323 loaded wagon arrivals and 68 loaded wagon departures. The inward loads included bagged urea for the CIBA-Geigy plant at Duxford, steel sheet from Shotton, insulating material from Stirling, seed potatoes from several locations in Scotland, furniture from Italy and onions from Spain. Among the outward loads were tractors for Ireland via Rosslare, military containers to Donnington, military vehicles to Ludgershall and herbicide to the Netherlands. The Class 08 pilot locomotive that serviced Cambridge Coalfields would also convey wagons to and from the Charringtons and Co-op coal depots and the Esso oil terminal at Coldhams Lane. A little further afield wagonload traffic was handled at Histon (imported fruit), Brookfields (coal for the cement works) and Fulbourn (grain). The Histon traffic was conveyed by the daily Fen Drayton sand train, while the Brookfields and Fulbourn flows shared a local trip working. Similar patterns of wagonload traffic could be found on many parts of the BR network.

Faced with mounting financial losses, BR closed down its traditional wagonload network to all traffic except coal and scrap metal in 1983 and completely in 1984. From then on all remaining wagonload flows were accommodated on the air-braked Speedlink network. That too failed to provide a long-term solution for the wagonload business, and it was to face the axe in 1991. However, for most of the Rail-blue period, BR was upbeat about the prospects of Speedlink, which it marketed as 'the freight name for reliability'.

BR's first move towards creating the Speedlink network had been the introduction early in 1973 of a daily wagonload service between Bristol and Glasgow. The traffic on that service was loaded in the latest design of railway-owned air-braked vans (later coded VAB) and open wagons (later OAA). Offering a transit time of 12 hours, the service attracted flows as diverse as tobacco, china clay, soap powder and newsprint; BR claimed that some 20% of the business was new to rail. A second air-braked wagonload service linked East Anglia with Edinburgh from October 1973.

The name 'Speedlink' was unveiled in 1977 by the then BR Chairman Peter (later Sir Peter) Parker. By that time more than 25 trunk services were operating daily, covering all major centres and with links to mainland Europe via the Dover– Dunkerque and Harwich–Zeebrugge train ferries.

The trains continued to use BR's new air-braked wagon fleet but increasingly carried privately owned stock as well, such as tank wagons for chemicals and covered hopper wagons for grain.

Although some Speedlink traffic was loaded and/or unloaded at railway-owned freight terminals, BR decided in the early 1980s to allow private operators to establish distribution terminals, some of which would eventually replace the railway-owned facilities altogether. Among the first privately owned distribution terminals were the Potter Group railheads at Ely and Selby, the Fogarty depot at Blackburn, the J. G. Russell depot at Glasgow Deanside and the P. D. Stirling depot at Mossend. These terminals became an integral part of the Speedlink network and dealt with a mixture of traffic similar to that handled by the railway-owned facilities.

Ominously, as the Speedlink network grew it became more complex and began to µresemble the old-fashioned vacuum-braked wagonload network that it was designed to replace. The period when the two networks were running side by side was particularly difficult, as vacuum-braked and air-braked wagons on the same route had to run either in separate trains — leading to wasteful duplication of resources — or else in the same train but with the brakes inoperative on either the vacuum-braked or the air-braked wagons, which meant lowering the train speed and providing a brake van at the rear.

Although they were not integrated within the wagonload network, BR ran a number of freight operations which involved intricate shunting and trip working and therefore did not fit into the trainload category. An example of this was Cornish china clay, its trains generally conveying a single type of traffic for a single customer but involving complex local movements between a number of different locations. South Wales coal also retained a large number of wagonload-style operations into the 1980s, using elderly vacuum-braked or even unfitted wagons to move various grades of coal between pits, washeries, blending sites, coking plants and ports.

The gradual decline of wagonload freight led to the closure of a number of remote railway outposts active for a long time after they lost their passenger service. Among the remarkable survivors was the Fakenham branch, where the daily pick-up goods train from Norwich could not complete its out-and-back journey in a single shift because of the time taken to operate the unmanned level crossings and shunt the various terminals on the route. Not until 1980 was the service cut back from Fakenham to Great Ryburgh.

Other rural branches that handled wagonload freight on borrowed time were Newcastle Emlyn (closed 1973), Wimborne (1977), Wadebridge (1978), Fraserburgh (1979), Louth (1980), Forfar and Meeth (both closed 1982). Several passenger branches also retained a pick-up freight service into the 1970s, among them Whitland–Pembroke Dock, Middlesbrough–Whitby and the Cambrian Coast line to Pwllheli.

Alongside the loss of railway infrastructure the BR traction fleet shrank significantly as the emphasis shifted from wagonload to trainload operation. Far fewer shunting locomotives were needed, and the axe fell first on non-standard types. Between 1967 and 1980 BR reduced its fleet of small shunters from 499 to just 62 examples. Some types, such as the Yorkshire Engine Co Class 02, the Drewry Class 04 and the Ruston & Hornsby Class 07, disappeared completely, while Classes 01 and 05 hung on by a thread, with just one survivor each. In Scotland a few short-wheelbase Barclay Class 06s were retained to work tightly curved freight lines such as the Dundee Harbour branch. The BR-built Class 03s were still fairly numerous in 1980, but their duties were being handed over wherever possible to the larger Class 08s. A few pre-Nationalisation shunters just made it into the blue era, but all were early targets for withdrawal.

As for main-line traction, the Western Region diesel-hydraulics were essentially mixed-traffic locomotives, but the decline of wagonload freight certainly made it easier for BR to rid itself of the problematic Class 22s and, in due course, the Class 35 'Hymeks'. Other lower-powered locomotive types which became less necessary because of the changes in freight traffic patterns included the British Thomson-Houston Class 15s, the Clayton Class 17s and the Metropolitan-Vickers 'Co-Bo' Class 28s. The entire fleet of centre-cab Class 14s — none of which received blue livery — was withdrawn by April 1969 as a direct consequence of freight cutbacks.

Later in the Rail-blue period the axe fell again on some of BR's lower-powered locomotives, including the Class 24s and Class 25s, which often worked in pairs on heavier freight duties. Of the more powerful diesel types the small fleet of Class 44 'Peaks' were all withdrawn by the end of 1980, and serious inroads started to be made into the Class 40 fleet in 1981. To replace the withdrawn types BR redeployed some locomotives without electric train-heating supply, notably the '45/0' and '47/0' sub-classes, from passenger to freight duties. But locomotives with electric train-heating supply could also work freight: there was no strict delineation between business sectors in those days.

BR's fleet of AC electric locomotives began life as mixed-traffic machines, but the Class 86s were divided in the early 1970s into passenger (Class 86/2) and freight (86/0) variants. Meanwhile the DC Class 76s were very much freight machines, working the freight-only Woodhead route. Although this was a fascinating stretch of railway with unique charm, its closure in 1981 was perhaps understandable: quite apart from the age of the equipment, even those freight services via Woodhead that supposedly ran as full trainloads were subjected to locomotive changes at each end of the electrified central section, adding significantly to the time taken and costs incurred.

Above: A Class 08 shunter draws a rake of air-braked steel wagons out of the up sorting sidings at Tees Yard on 19 March 1981, while two further Class 08s await their next move. On the left is the 'van kip', a pair of inclined sidings where brake vans were held ready to be attached to the rear of departing trains. *Paul Shannon*

Below: The remaining Class 17 'Claytons' had less than a year before withdrawal when No 8567 was photographed leaving Cadder Yard with a trip freight to Motherwell on 14 April 1971. Most 'Claytons' were to be scrapped within a few years of their withdrawal, leaving just No 8568 to survive in preservation. *Derek Cross*

Left: Hardly a taxing load for Class 52 'Western' No D1045 *Western Viscount*, climbing Rattery Bank, west of Totnes, with the afternoon Exeter–Truro freight on 11 September 1973. *David Rapson*

Below left: 'Hymek' No D7033 takes the Taunton station-avoiding line after leaving Fairwater Yard with an up mixed freight on 29 April 1970. The number '8' in the headcode denotes a partly fitted freight, and this is confirmed by the livery of the wagons — bauxite for the fitted minerals and hoppers at the front of the train, and grey for the unfitted hoppers at the rear. *Bernard Mills*

Above: Class 25 locomotives gained a foothold in the West Country in 1971 following BR's decision to phase out the non-standard hydraulics. At Hemyock on 20 September 1974 No 25 052 shunts the six-wheeled milk tanks that (despite the headcode displayed!) will form the 7B70 trip working to Tiverton Junction. *David Rapson*

Below: The railway carried coal not just from collieries to power stations but also to and from washeries, coking plants, blending sites and concentration depots. No 37 258 makes its way along the Maesteg branch with the 9B93 trip working from Margam on 15 April 1982. The five MDO wagons are all loaded with washed coal for Maesteg coal-concentration depot — two wagons from Onllwyn, one from Coedbach and two from Cynheidre. *Paul Shannon*

Above: The Hemyock branch closed to passengers in September 1963 and to general freight two years later, but milk traffic from the dairy at Hemyock kept this delightful rural backwater alive until 1975. Class 22 No D6333 shunts milk tanks at the terminus on 19 April 1969. *Bernard Mills*

Below: In charge of train 7S38, the 11.05 from St Blazey to Glasgow, Class 52 No 1049 *Western Monarch* passes the Unigate milk depot at Lostwithiel on 20 September 1974. The train comprises a fine mixture of rolling stock, including ventilated vans, a gunpowder van, bitumen tanks, wooden-bodied open wagons, air-braked vans and, just before the brake van, some unfitted mineral wagons. *Brian Roberts*

Above: 'Peak' No 45 077 passes Totnes on 28 September 1979 with an up fitted freight conveying mainly china clay in UCV and OWV wagons bound for the Potteries. This traffic was to go over to air-braked operation with new covered hopper wagons in 1982. In the siding on the up side are milk tanks, which were still in regular use at that time. *Paul Shannon*

Below: In the 1950s BR introduced more than 20,000 two-axle 'Conflat' wagons to carry 'door-to-door'-type containers between station goods yards. A good number of 'door-to-door' containers are included in this up mixed freight, passing Cholsey on 29 April 1976 behind No 47 156. *Brian Roberts*

Left: A sole example of the Hunslet 0-6-0 shunter fleet, which was introduced in 1955 and originally totalled 69 locomotives, remained in use on the Isle of Wight until 1981 to haul permanent-way trains. No 05 001 is seen stabled at Sandown in summer 1978. *D. J. Hayes*

Centre left: Scottish manufacturer Andrew Barclay supplied BR with 35 0-4-0 locomotives for light shunting and trip freight work in Scotland. They became Class 06 for TOPS purposes, but only 10 examples survived long enough to receive their TOPS number. No 06 008 is pictured at an unknown location on 27 August 1978. *Ian Allan Library*

Below: No 13 001, one of the three 'master and slave' shunters created from the permanent coupling of pairs of Class 08s, is pictured at Tinsley depot on 9 April 1978. Apart from their distinctive appearance, the Class 13s were unusual in being fitted with cab signalling apparatus and two-way radio telephones to improve the efficiency of hump shunting at Tinsley yard. *Hugh Ballantyne*

Right: Southampton Docks produced enough wagonload freight to warrant the building of a dedicated fleet of 14 diesel-electric shunting locomotives, later known as Class 07. No 07 003 rests at Eastleigh on 29 March 1975. Within two years wagonload traffic in the docks had dwindled to nothing and BR had no further use for the Class 07s; the last examples were withdrawn in July 1977. Most saw further use in private ownership and six have been preserved. *David Rapson*

Below right: Class 03 shunters with cut-down cabs were provided for coal trains on the Burry Port & Gwendraeth Valley line, with its restricted clearances. Nos 03 141, 03 119 and 03 152 haul a rake of HTV hopper wagons down the valley about one mile south of Cwmmawr on 7 September 1983. All three of these Class 03s have since been preserved; at the time of writing they are based on the Pontypool & Blaenavon Railway, the West Somerset Railway and the Swindon & Cricklade Railway respectively. *Hugh Ballantyne*

Above: Many hundreds of two-axle ventilated vans disappeared from the railway network as BR's sundries and general merchandise traffic gradually ebbed away. At Edge Hill Park sidings on 2 October 1974 No 25 297 stands coupled to a rake of ventilated vans forming the 'T21' trip working to the National Carriers Ltd depot at Huskisson. The vertical white stripes on the first two vans indicate that these vehicles were fitted with shock-absorbers. *David Rapson*

Below: Not the kind of load that the Class 50s were designed for: No 50 022 comes off the Lymm line at Skelton Junction with a trip working conveying coal to Partington on 30 May 1974. The train would run round in the loop just east of Skelton Junction before taking the Partington line. Just six years old at the time of the photograph, the locomotive was destined to spend the majority of its career on the Western Region, ultimately being withdrawn in 1989. *Brian Roberts*

Above: Having just crossed the River Dee, No 40118 enters Hawarden Bridge station with train 8F13, the 08.42 from Croes Newydd to Dee Marsh Junction, on 21 May 1979. Behind the hooded steel-carriers are mineral wagons which would have carried scrap metal to Shotton steelworks. The blast furnaces at Shotton would cease production in the following year. *David Rapson*

Below: Nos 25 297 and 25 287 pass Manchester Victoria with an eastbound train of track panels on 'Salmon' wagons on 25 July 1979. At this time both locomotives were allocated to Wigan Springs Branch depot; they would be withdrawn in 1986 and 1985 respectively. *Paul Shannon*

Above: As wagonload freight declined so too did traditional marshalling yards, and those that survived often handled mainly railway-infrastructure traffic. Still in its long-obsolete blue livery, No 08 799 shunts ZBA 'Rudd' infrastructure wagons at Temple Mills yard on 29 October 1998. *Paul Shannon*

Below: Whitemoor Yard was an important node for wagonload freight traffic to and from East Anglia. In 1981 it still handled more than 3,000 wagons a week, despite closure of the hump the previous year. Pilot locomotive No 08 526 draws a motley selection of new and old wagons out of the south end of the yard on 13 January 1981. Today the site of Whitemoor Yard is occupied by a rail-served 'virtual quarry', operated by First GB Railfreight on behalf of Network Rail. *Paul Shannon*

Above: The Class 73 electro-diesels regularly worked inter-regional freight trains via Kensington Olympia. No 73 002, one of six pre-production examples delivered in 1962, approaches Olympia on 19 April 1982 with household coal from Acton to Wimbledon. At this time Olympia still had a mixture of lower- and upper-quadrant semaphore signals, but these would soon be replaced by colour lights. *Paul Shannon*

Below: With track-remodelling in progress in the yard, No 31 142 leaves Cambridge with the 8J75 wagonload feeder service to Whitemoor on 5 May 1981. The train includes a mixture of air-braked SPA plate wagons and vacuum-braked stock, the incompatibility of these two braking systems dictating the use of a brake van. *Paul Shannon*

Above: The Midland Railway signalbox and former goods shed provide a nostalgic setting for Nos 20 059 and 20 210 as they pass Whitwell with a southbound engineers' train on 15 April 1983. On the right is the access line to Whitwell Colliery, with a rake of merry-go-round hoppers awaiting collection. Today Whitwell Colliery is a distant memory and through freight traffic is sparse, but the line is kept busy with the restored 'Robin Hood line' passenger service.
Paul Shannon

Below: The freight-only Bolsover branch once served two collieries as well as the Coalite plant at Bolsover. On 15 June 1981 No 20 211 passes Markham Colliery sidings with the evening 'T94' trip working from Bolsover to Barrow Hill, comprising mainly unfitted MCO mineral wagons. Both Markham and Bolsover collieries were to close in 1993, but production at the Coalite plant would continue until 2004.
Paul Shannon

Above: After cutting their teeth on express passenger duties the 10 original 'Peaks' settled down to a career of unglamorous freight work based at Toton depot. No 44 007 *Ingleborough* heads north between Avenue Sidings and Hasland with the 18.01 Spondon–Tinsley mixed freight on 18 July 1978. This locomotive was one of the last three Class 44s to remain in service, being officially withdrawn in November 1980. *Brian Roberts*

Below: For many years the Bedford–Bletchley line, with its semaphore signals and manual signalboxes, remained something of a railway backwater. Freight traffic included 'Fletliner' brick trains from Stewartby, containerised refuse trains to Stewartby and spent ballast to the tip at Lidlington. No 25 088 approaches Stewartby station on its way back to Bletchley depot after a local freight duty on 28 July 1981. *Paul Shannon*

Above: A typical mixed freight train on the Settle–Carlisle line passes Stainforth on 27 August 1974 behind Class 40 No 40 008. The consist includes standard ventilated vans, gunpowder vans (recognisable by their lower roof height), mineral wagons, various empty steel carriers, a flat wagon loaded with a road vehicle, and at least one wagon carrying a 'door-to-door' container. *David Rapson*

Below: The steel and chemical industries along the south bank of the Tees estuary assured a steady stream of freight traffic between Middlesbrough and Redcar. No 31 285 passes South Bank coke ovens with girders from British Steel Lackenby to Tees Yard on 25 March 1982. Earlier in the day it had hauled trip workings from Tees Yard to Wilton with lime and from Tees Yard to South Bank with coal, in each case returning with empty wagons. *Paul Shannon*

Above: Still with headcode panel, No 37 242 passes Ferryhill with the 8K84 wagonload service from Tyne Yard to Tees Yard on 8 June 1982. The '37' was to end its working career as a Sandite locomotive in 1999, being then bought for preservation but later scrapped. *Paul Shannon*

Below: In the 1960s Tinsley Yard was wired up to allow through electric operation to and from the Woodhead route. No 76 051, one of the few Class 76s not equipped for multiple operation, leaves Tinsley with the 'T30' trip working to Deepcar on 23 September 1980. *Paul Shannon*

Above: The Steetley magnesia works at Hartlepool received lime and dolime (calcined dolomite) from Thrislington in PAA and PAB covered hopper wagons. No 47 360 awaits departure from Hartlepool with empty wagons for Thrislington on 18 July 1986, operating as local trip working 6P62. On the left is a Transfesa ferry wagon which would have been used to transport the finished product — refractory-grade magnesia — from Hartlepool. *Paul Shannon*

Below: Spekeland Road became the main public freight terminal for Merseyside in the 1980s, handling steel and other products for local distribution. Pilot locomotive No 08 809 is seen stabled at Spekeland Road on 2 April 1986, coupled to a rake of coil carriers that had come from Allied Steel & Wire at Cardiff via the Speedlink network. *Paul Shannon*

Above: The Speedlink feeder service on the Cumbrian Coast line carried mainly chemical products to and from Corkickle, for the Albright & Wilson works, and rails from Workington. No 40 082 crosses Eskmeals Viaduct with a typical mixture of wagons forming train 6O38, the 17.14 from Workington to Dover, on 13 July 1983. This train called at several yards *en route*, and it was rare for any wagons to travel all the way from Workington to Dover. *Paul Shannon*

Below: Passing Wednesbury on the freight-only line from Stourbridge Junction to Bescot is No 47 330 with train 6M72, the 22.15 St Blazey–Cliffe Vale Speedlink service, on 18 August 1989. The vans at the rear of the train would be detached at Bescot Yard, leaving the 'Tiger' china-clay carriers to continue to Cliffe Vale. No 47 330 would later be included in the Class 57 conversion programme, becoming No 57 312 *The Hood* in 2003. *Paul Shannon*

Above: More than 90 Rail-blue-liveried Class 08 shunters made it into the 21st century. With its double-arrow logo painted out, No 08 495 arrives at Doncaster Belmont Yard with intermodal wagons from Doncaster Railport on 24 April 2001. At this time Belmont Yard was a busy hub for EWS wagonload traffic. *Paul Shannon*

Below: Mossend Euroterminal was established on the site of Mossend Up Yard as the Channel Tunnel intermodal terminal serving Scotland. The level of Channel Tunnel business was disappointing, but for a time the terminal produced a regular flow to and from Paris and a handful of other European centres. No 08 670 shunts Paris traffic at Mossend on 14 July 1998. *Paul Shannon*